Matthew

Matthew
The Gospel of Promised Blessings

Matthew
978-1-7910-3013-1
978-1-7910-3015-5 *eBook*

Matthew: DVD
978-1-7910-3014-8

Matthew: Leader Guide
978-1-7910-3016-2
978-1-7910-3017-9 *eBook*

Also by Matthew L. Skinner

Acts: Catching up with the Spirit

MATTHEW L. SKINNER

Matthew

The Gospel of Promised Blessings

Abingdon Press | Nashville

Matthew
The Gospel of Promised Blessings

Library of Congress Control Number: 2023952076
978-1-7910-3013-1

Cover Image: James B. Janknegt (b. 1953), *World's Smallest Seed*, 2011, Oil on Canvas, 40 x 30 inch, https://www.bcartfarm.com/.

MANUFACTURED IN THE UNITED STATES OF AMERICA

*Dedicated with love and gratitude to
the congregation and staff of
Westminster Presbyterian Church
in Minneapolis.*

*In your company I experience so much joy in
teaching, learning, dreaming, struggling,
worshipping, helping, and healing.*

Contents

Preface

For well over 1900 years the Gospel according to Matthew, like the other three Gospels in the New Testament, has preserved memories about Jesus, his actions, and his teachings. Those memories, which the Gospel's author tied together into a single story, sustained ancient Christians and instructed new generations of the church about what it means to experience, trust, and follow Jesus Christ. Matthew continues to influence Christian theology and practices even today. If you know the Lord's Prayer (also called the Our Father), Matthew is partially responsible. If you played one of the magi (also referred to as wise men or kings in some settings) in a Christmas pageant, you can thank Matthew for including those characters. If you wonder why some professed Christians are so preoccupied with threatening others about the horrors of hell, we need to admit that some of their inspiration comes from Matthew. Rather, I'd say that those people take their inspiration mostly from misinterpretations of Matthew, a defective view of God's grace, and probably the rage they carry. But let's not jump too far ahead of ourselves. We're still only in the first paragraph of the preface. Let's give Matthew the benefit of the doubt while we get started.

Matthew plays a part in how Christians talk about their faith, whether they've read it or not. That means the book that appears first in the New Testament is too important to leave unread. Likewise, Matthew's emphasis on certain topics and distinctive characteristics of Jesus is too weighty to ignore. I've written this book, therefore, to introduce or reintroduce you to one of the most influential Christian writings ever produced.

Matthew plays a part in how Christians talk about their faith, whether they've read it or not.

My main intention isn't to lead you into a deeper understanding of Matthew, although I'm confident that will happen. My chief goal, instead, is that your willingness to engage Matthew seriously and honestly will broaden your imagination about what it means for you to play a part in the mercy and restoration that Jesus promises to bring to the world. I hope to illuminate Matthew and draw you further inside so you'll have some questions answered and also generate new ones. From my professional experiences—as a seminary professor, a creator of resources for preachers, and a teacher in a local congregation—I'm convinced that entering into conversation with the Bible and even wrangling with its uncomfortable parts are always worth the effort. Doing so can lead us to expect more from God and spur us to dedicate ourselves more energetically to Jesus's ongoing commitment to transform the world.

Even though they all center around the same historical person named Jesus, every Gospel tells its story in its own way. I want to respect Matthew's own point of view and the integrity of the narrative this Gospel puts before us. I'll refrain, therefore, from speculating about questions that Matthew can't answer, like what happened during Jesus's teenage years. We won't wander into more complicated questions, such as trying to determine whether an episode in Matthew describes *exactly* what really happened at a certain time in Jesus's life. I want us instead to dwell deeply in how this one particular Gospel remembers him. Along the way, we'll explore how Matthew's distinctive memories have influenced our understanding of Christian faith and life—both to appreciate what has proved helpful and to acknowledge where harm has resulted.

I don't expect you to agree with everything I have to say about Matthew, although I won't be disappointed if you do. I'll be happier if, instead, this book generates curiosity and conversations about what Matthew has to say and what it means for us to take Matthew's depiction of Jesus seriously today.

As Matthew presents the good news to us in its own voice, we will encounter Jesus promising to bless a wide array of people, especially those whose lives appear far from blessed. Jesus, in Matthew, promises that change is afoot. He likewise appears fond of telling stories about things that grow, vulnerable creatures finding shelter, people who give and receive generously, and the joy that springs up when we discover something amazing. May your encounter with Matthew have similar effects for you.

Introduction

It never fails to happen. Every three years in November I receive emails about the Gospel according to Matthew, and they make me smile. Preachers, most of whom were once students in my seminary classroom, write to ask if I can recommend anything to help them make sense of Matthew. "Any new books out there? Any good insights?" I think they hope someone made a breakthrough or found a scroll with all the answers buried in a cave somewhere. At the same time, I understand the dread in their words. I share their concerns.

First, I chuckle. Don't I always tell students that the Bible isn't easy? Sometimes you have to wrestle with it to get a better perspective.

Let me explain. The Revised Common Lectionary, a resource that assigns biblical passages for congregations to read throughout the church's year, follows a three-year cycle. Every time the cycle renews, at the beginning of every third Advent, congregations that follow this widely used lectionary encounter a passage from Matthew on almost every Sunday for a full year. And Matthew, you see, is notorious for producing mixed feelings, probably more so than any other Gospel. A lot of preachers, who generally are people who like to focus on God's generosity and Jesus's good news, tremble.

When I reply to the emails, I stand up for Matthew before acknowledging the difficult parts. Without this Gospel, we wouldn't have Jesus's famous Sermon on the Mount. Plus, it's one of the two Gospels (Luke is the other) that makes a strong effort to highlight Jesus's parables—short, quirky, illustrative stories like the one about a dense tree that grows from a tiny mustard seed and provides a safe habitat for birds. Parables indicate that Jesus wants people to think and imagine, not simply to have information spoon-fed to them. Also, what about Matthew's story of the courageous magi who journey with gifts to honor Jesus after his birth and then have to outmaneuver evil King Herod? What a great reminder of Christmas's strangely subversive qualities!

But Matthew tells a bigger and often harder story. That's why the emails come. Everyone I know who preaches or teaches about Matthew recognizes the challenges. An anger courses through Matthew, expressing itself in harsh language and disingenuous caricatures of people who oppose Jesus. Over the centuries, many Christians have mined Matthew to gather fuel for their antisemitic ire. In addition, Jesus threatens judgment and punishment frequently in Matthew. It can be tricky for a preacher to assure a congregation that God is love when the Scripture reading for a given Sunday talks about casting someone "into the eternal fire."

Since you're still reading, I assume you're still interested in Matthew. I am. It's an occasionally challenging book to understand, for reasons I've mentioned and more. At the same time, it presents us with a depiction of Jesus that overflows with relentless kindness, profound concern for those who suffer, stunning gentleness, and abundant grace. Jesus promises blessings and delivers them. Yet Matthew also presents Jesus as a controversial figure in a contentious landscape. Matthew emphasizes that Jesus's followers should expect to find themselves likewise in difficult conditions. Faith does not come easily. The false promises that compete with Jesus's promises are seductive, but hollow. The world has to change, otherwise mercy will be overrun and justice will never arrive. The people who most need relief from the cruelties of the world won't receive it if Jesus's followers get distracted from what matters. The stakes are extremely high in Matthew's account; accordingly, Jesus comes across as impassioned and achingly urgent. This Gospel tells the story in a way that urges readers to opt for Jesus and embrace his vision, avoiding anything that can knock them from the path he sets before them.

The stakes are extremely high in Matthew's account; accordingly, Jesus comes across as impassioned and achingly urgent.

Studying Matthew will help us learn more about Jesus and more about how this Gospel might have influenced the people who first read it in the early generations of the church. But exploring Matthew will also lead us to consider our own faith. Our journey into Matthew will prompt us to ask productive, worthwhile questions. What does it mean to follow the same Jesus who promises to accompany his people? What is the purpose of the Christian church? Which dimensions of our inherited Christian tradition align or do not align with what this Gospel really says? Matthew deserves our attention.

Where Matthew Came From

No Gospel ever intended to say *everything* that could be said about Jesus. Each Gospel tells its story to reassure, galvanize, correct, or convince readers, and that raises questions for us about who the Gospels' ancient audiences might have been, what their circumstances were, and how a specific Gospel might have influenced them. We can say nearly the same thing in a different way: every Gospel tells us something about Jesus, of course, but also every Gospel tells us something about the memories that some of his followers held on to decades after his life, death, and resurrection. Matthew could have relayed more information about Jesus and could have emphasized different aspects of his teachings. Nevertheless, the episodes Matthew narrates and the themes that recur reveal this Gospel's interest in reassuring some people, criticizing others, and equipping still others for the journey ahead of them. What can we observe in Matthew itself about the issues that influenced the way it tells its story?

The text of Matthew never identifies its author or describes what was happening when it was first put into written form. Later Christian writers connected this Gospel to one of Jesus's close followers, a man named Matthew (9:9). It's impossible to prove or disprove that. I don't think we would read Matthew much differently, however, if we knew for sure that a certain disciple wrote it or if we somehow decided it was written by someone else. The story is what it is.

Most credible scholars conclude Matthew was written during the last two decades of the first century, at least fifty years after Jesus's death and resurrection, roughly 80–100 CE. At that time, the Jerusalem Temple was in ruins, destroyed by Roman forces in 70 CE. The catastrophic loss of the temple effectively meant the loss of the priesthood and temple rituals, so Jews found themselves in the position of reshaping or reforming what it entailed for them to practice Judaism. It was a fertile time of religious reorientation. Also during that time, cracks began to widen between churches and synagogues. Christian faith originated within Judaism; Jesus and his first followers were all Jewish and not intending to create a separate religion. During the first decades of the Christian church's existence, it seems that Jews who embraced Jesus as the Messiah or the Christ (the two titles are synonyms) lived and practiced their faith relatively harmoniously among Jews who did not share those beliefs about Jesus. Over time, and especially around the point when the temple was lost, the harmony began to break down for reasons too complex to trace here. By the early second century CE, the division was pretty much complete.

I'm convinced that Matthew carries in itself the tensions that strained some predominantly Jewish communities as the harmony was eroding. That's not a controversial or unpopular opinion among New Testament scholars. In the ways that Matthew presents Jesus and in the themes that stand out, we can detect the pain and frustration that arose as groups of Christ-followers (composed mostly of people who also were Jewish) contended with other Jewish groups over questions about who rightly interpreted Jewish law and tradition. Matthew reflects the point of view of people who attached their full allegiance to Jesus. Through Jesus, Matthew insists, a new reality for humanity will emerge, accomplished by the God of Israel. Knowing not everyone agrees, Matthew tries to make a case for Jesus that proceeds in at least two ways: celebrating Jesus on his own merits, and setting Jesus and his teachings sharply against other leaders who have different ideas for how Judaism should move forward.

Many passages in Matthew instruct readers about coexisting with people who aren't quite right in how they believe or hope. That suggests Matthew would have appealed especially to believers who found themselves in conflict with other believers over questions about observing Jewish law or maintaining certain standards of Christian conduct. The influx and behavior of Gentiles (non-Jews) in some Christian communities might have also intensified disagreements among churches or especially between churches and other groups of Jews. In any case, suspicion is in the air in Matthew, and so stories about dealing with discord and distrust loom large. Imagine separate groups of religious people clashing about which of them and their beliefs rightly describe how God might be known and how God might be in the process of setting the world right. As we know, those kinds of disputes, whether ancient or modern, generate a lot of heat.

Most communities of faith engage in lively debates about religious belief, the ground of people's religious identity, fostering friendly fellowship, honoring traditions, and anticipating the future. When those debates grow more fierce, conflict takes a toll on communities and on people's ability to trust their neighbors. Folks cling to grudges and make extra effort to root out falsehoods. Earlier I noted an angry streak that emerges from time to time in Matthew. That would fit scenarios where escalating friction had frayed people's nerves and perhaps traumatized their minds and bodies. Experiences like those understandably influence how people think about God, themselves, and others. Matthew tells a story about Jesus that means to equip people who were navigating difference, rivalries, and polarizing quarrels.

Matthew proclaims Jesus as the Jewish Messiah, sent by God to the Jewish people to inaugurate what he refers to as "the kingdom of heaven." Jesus's Jewishness is evident in his teaching, values, and merciful actions. The Gospel's keen attention to Jewish traditions and the law of Moses, as well as its frequent citations of passages from Jewish scripture (also, now, the Christian Old Testament) prompts some to refer to Matthew as the most Jewish of the four Gospels. Matthew also depicts Jesus delivering harsh criticism to Jewish Pharisees and other religious leaders. The book has no patience for people who embrace different teachings or who don't believe in Jesus the way they supposedly should. Some, therefore, refer to Matthew as the most anti-Jewish of the four Gospels. They mean that Matthew promotes a way of remembering Jesus that actively seeks to discredit other expressions of Jewish teachings and practices. Matthew certainly has been called upon to speak that way during the church's long history.

The Intensities Flowing through Matthew

It's safe to conclude that the energy driving Jesus's teachings and actions was an unflinching conviction that God is on the verge of shaking up the human condition and instituting something new and wonderful. The theme that arises most frequently in Matthew—as well as in Mark and Luke, yet to a lesser extent in John—concerns the arrival of that new reality: God's "kingdom."

"Kingdom" is the traditional way of translating a Greek term that means "reign" or "rule." "Kingdom" in English implies a new place or country. "Reign" in English more accurately keeps the focus on the action of the one ruling, the one who sets the standards and protects the inhabitants. Jesus, therefore, announces a state of affairs in which *God's* intentions have sway. This new reign emerges when God activates God's graciousness within human society, reordering our values and ushering in wholeness, health, and security. With Jesus's arrival, this new state of affairs "has come near" (4:17). He inaugurates the Kingdom, although it remains in transit, still in the process of breaking through in all its fullness. Jesus situates himself on the cusp of a new era in how God will be present to the world and for the sake of the world.

Only in Matthew does Jesus speak of the "kingdom of heaven," although every now and then "kingdom of God" also appears. Both phrases refer to the same thing, with "heaven" working synonymously for "God." In this book, to avoid confusion, I'll keep the traditional language of "Kingdom" instead of "reign," since most Bible translations still use it. It's up to you to remember that Jesus's use of "Kingdom" refers to a new society breaking in and God altering a status quo that we might have thought could never be changed. He imagines it *here*, not in a far-off paradise. The point is, with all of Jesus's talk about a Kingdom in which conventional expectations for what's right, what's fair, and what's possible get rewritten, Jesus lets us know that he perceives everything differently. The passion behind his desire to share his vision for how the world should operate is consuming and tenacious. It makes him come across as . . . honestly . . . intense.

All the Gospels, each in its own way, portray Jesus smoldering with a determined intensity.

All the Gospels, each in its own way, portray Jesus smoldering with a determined intensity. It emerges in various ways, such as when he faces off with the authorities in the days before his arrest, berates his opponents, issues warnings to those who harm innocent people, and cautions his followers about travails they'll face. We in the church often try to file the sharp edges off Jesus, because they make us uncomfortable and are easily exploited by religious extremists. In the end, however, the Jesus of the Gospels remains restless. He resists our desires for him to mellow out.

Matthew creates challenges because much of Jesus's intensity in this Gospel comes across either as anger or as him threatening to make others suffer for their waywardness. It's fair to call Matthew an occasionally irate Gospel, in that Jesus sometimes seems to have no patience or grace for certain actions or people.

Matthew's intensity doesn't mean to bully us. Remember, it's a book that urges readers to choose Jesus and keep their trust fixed on him. As Matthew tells it, a choice needs to be made, and that choice comes across as all the more urgent because the world is a duplicitous place and many counterfeit assurances vie for our attention. Matthew also lifts up the importance of the church but doesn't want the church to embrace Jesus in ways that make it self-satisfied. A perennial challenge for us who follow Jesus involves espousing the urgency of his promised blessings without becoming intolerant, unwelcoming, or obnoxious.

Jesus's basic intensity shouldn't surprise us. Visionaries in any era who see the world plainly for the broken place it is and imagine new, appealing possibilities often can't contain their frustration. The frustration sometimes lashes out at people who can't perceive what the visionary does. It can arise from knowing the massive piles of injustice and opposition that stand in the way.

When Jesus's intensity rises to the surface in Matthew, we may be tempted to take those passages as contradicting or negating the more comforting things he says and does. Understanding this Gospel well requires us to realize that Jesus's aggravations and warnings instead reveal the magnitude of his compassion and his desire to shelter the people who most need sheltering.

Introduction

Jesus has more to say about judgment and punishment in Matthew than he does in the other three Gospels. Almost all of the writers we encounter in the New Testament nevertheless make some kind of reference to a culminating judgment. They all regard Jesus as, among other things, God's designated agent to judge the world and do justice. Our actions have consequences, and God expects obedience and goodwill from us. Jesus will be the means by which God sorts out the world's shortcomings and fixes the problems humanity creates. What exactly that will look like is described differently in different biblical books.

No biblical book includes as many references to "hell" as Matthew does. The Greek word in question is *Gehenna*, which comes from the Hebrew name for a valley outside Jerusalem. Prior to the Babylonian Exile (sixth century BCE), *Gehenna* was a site where some people would sacrifice children (using fire) and engage in other abominable cultic practices to satisfy foreign gods. By the time Jesus was born, the term understandably had come to connote evil and was used to designate a place for punishing evildoers in the afterlife.

Matthew doesn't include detailed descriptions of what Jesus means by *Gehenna*, but two references speak of "the *Gehenna* of fire" (5:22; 18:9). In other passages Jesus doesn't mention hell but talks of people suffering "weeping and gnashing of teeth," "outer darkness," "eternal fire," and other images that you don't want the preacher to mention on the day you invite your new neighbors to church.

If suddenly you're worried you bought the wrong book, stay with me. I bring up this topic to point out that Matthew is one of the few New Testament writings that have contributed to Christian imagery about hell and punishment, as theologians through the centuries eventually developed their more expansive doctrines of judgment and retribution. The other books include 2 Thessalonians, Jude, and Revelation (no surprise there!). In other words, dwelling on hell is not a concern of most biblical authors. We can talk about divine judgment without it involving harsh punishment or eternal torment. Furthermore, the biblical books that do mention punishment have little to say beyond symbols that illustrate destruction and sorrow.

We have been overly influenced, however, by traditions that emerged after the Bible. Later thinkers such as Dante Alighieri, in his fourteenth-century work *Inferno*, which is part of his Divine Comedy, are responsible for the detailed visions of punishment that make your skin crawl and feed the assumptions that countless people make about hell and the afterlife. Search for the fifteenth-century Beaune Altarpiece ("The Last Judgment") online and observe the painting's awful rendering of an emotionless Jesus overseeing souls weighed in scales to determine who goes to heaven or hell. Imagine being fed a steady diet of those themes every time you go to church. I guess that's one reason—but hardly the only reason—why wild-eyed individuals choose to walk around Times Square waving signs reading "Turn or burn!" Add all of this to the list of things that must frustrate Jesus on a daily basis.

Notions of hell as eternal torment have led the church in very unhelpful directions when it comes to making sense of what Jesus says about judgment in Matthew. Yet we can't read Matthew and not discuss judgment.

I'm not denying that Matthew's focus on judgment is unpleasant; I'm saying we shouldn't overlook it. Considering judgment will help us get inside the Gospel's impassioned promises about blessings. My agenda isn't to make Matthew's bitter verses more palatable. It is to offer ways of navigating this intense story about Jesus. Then we can consider how Matthew's intensities align or clash with the ways we speak about God, the good news of Jesus Christ, and the human condition.

We can read Matthew's bitter verses in more productive and accurate ways. Many parts of this Gospel promise punishment for some. Those passages sound cruel, especially at first glance. We'll investigate several of the relevant passages and consider whether we can or should reconcile the images of a God who pours out love and blessing with images of a God who promises judgment to come. Are love and judgment utterly incompatible? I believe they are not—not if we understand what those things mean to Jesus, as Matthew presents him.

Overview of Matthew

I recommend you read all of Matthew before you go too deep into this book. Having a basic grasp of the full narrative will help you keep track of where the individual passages that I'll discuss fit into the Gospel's overall scheme. Try to read Matthew like you read other stories, paying attention to how the parts influence your sense of the whole and vice versa. All sorts of mischief arises when people build a theology—their overall conceptions of God, humanity, and Jesus's good news—around just an isolated verse, a single passage, or a lone theme. Let the whole book tell its story in all of its beauty and sometimes strangeness.

Matthew begins with a genealogy of Jesus and tales about his birth and early childhood. Avoiding multiple threats, his family eventually takes him to Nazareth in Galilee, where he grows up.

When Jesus is an adult, he presents himself to John the Baptist for baptism, at which point God's Spirit comes to him and sends him into the wilderness. Jesus resists various tests the devil places before him and relocates to Capernaum on the shore of the Sea of Galilee. Once he learns that the authorities have arrested John the Baptist, he begins proclaiming the arrival of the kingdom of heaven.

Jesus conducts a public ministry marked by teaching, tangible acts of mercy and miraculous healing, exorcism of unclean spirits, criticism of certain religious leaders, and warnings about resisting God's emerging kingdom. He gravitates toward people known for their dubious reputations and calls people to follow him and participate in his ministry.

Beginning in 16:13 the narrative takes a turn when Jesus begins to talk about his upcoming arrest, suffering, death, and resurrection. The prospect of his arrival in Jerusalem heightens the dreadful anticipation. Some of his followers witness his appearance transfigured and hear God, speaking from a cloud, reaffirm Jesus's identity as the Son of God. The narrative now focuses less on miracles and healings and more on Jesus's instructions about how his followers should conduct themselves.

Jesus finally arrives at the outskirts of Jerusalem in 21:1. Matthew 21–25 describes him teaching in the city, frustrating some religious leaders, appealing to the crowds, and offering several parables and warnings about being prepared for what the future will bring.

After Jesus shares a Passover meal with a group of his closest followers, the local authorities arrest him during the night, interrogate him, and bring him before Pilate, the leading Roman official in the region. Pilate condemns Jesus to execution by crucifixion.

In Matthew's final chapter, two women named Mary, followers of Jesus, observe an angel unsealing Jesus's tomb. They meet the resurrected Jesus, who instructs them to arrange a reunion in Galilee. There, Jesus commissions his followers to carry on his ministry and be confident in his enduring presence with them.

The skeleton of Matthew's plot may sound familiar to you, for it resembles the plot of Luke's Gospel and especially Mark's Gospel. The general outline of John is similar, too. Most scholars conclude that the author of Matthew constructed this narrative using Mark as a source and framework. A very large proportion of what appears in Mark also appears in Matthew. Additionally, Matthew includes much material that came from other sources, both written and orally preserved memories about Jesus. Approximately one quarter of Matthew consists of stories about Jesus that appear in no other known Gospel. If not for Matthew, we wouldn't have them.

Introduction

I've chosen not to organize this book as a stroll through Matthew in sequence from its opening verses to its final scene. Instead, we'll jump around the Gospel, exploring specific passages and noticing various themes. As a result, I will skip over some parts of Matthew. It's a long Gospel. I won't say much, for example, about Jesus's birth or his crucifixion. The baptism, the transfiguration, many miracles, and Jesus's predictions of his death and resurrection will also miss the cut. Obviously those are important pieces of Matthew's story, so let me refer you to a meaty study Bible or the books I recommend in the "For Further Reading" section if you want to explore them.

In the chapters ahead, I'll give preference especially to action, teaching, and topics that either appear only in Matthew or have a distinctive "Matthew-like" quality about them. You'll learn to speak Matthew's language, so to speak, and get inside its perspective. You'll gain a clearer sense of why this Gospel offers such an intensely passionate portrait of Jesus and his transformational vision for the world and the church. You'll know where to find the refreshing blessings Jesus promises.

Whether you're sitting down with Matthew for the first time or the fiftieth, this way of exploring it will help you understand what makes it a delight to read, a challenge to read, and sometimes both at once.

My approach won't explain every word of the Gospel—as if I could!—but it will encourage you to consider how Matthew, even with its intense parts, might nourish, challenge, and reorient your faith. Whether you're sitting down with Matthew for the first time or the fiftieth, this way of exploring it will help you understand what makes it a delight to read, a challenge to read, and sometimes both at once.

If you don't believe me about that, ask a preacher what they think.

Chapter 1

Promised Blessings

Passages to Explore:

Matthew 5:1-12   (Blessed Are ...)
Matthew 6:30-33   (Promises for Those of Little Faith)
Matthew 20:1-16   (Workers in the Vineyard)
Matthew 25:31-46   (Sheep and Goats)

I remember one of my professors saying, "A lot of people read the Bible and assume the first question they need to answer is, 'Based on this passage, what should I do? How should I act?'" He urged us to think differently: "A better way of approaching the Bible is to ask, 'What does this text promise?'" He was passing along good wisdom. The Bible is full of promises—some explicit, most implicit. Instead of treating it as a rule book or a history book, try to absorb what it claims to be true. What is God like? How does God operate? What can we expect for the future? Sit with questions like those first. You might decide to act differently as a result, but that happens down the road.

We begin our exploration of Matthew, then, with passages that show us Jesus making bold promises—declarations about what he will do, where he will be, the kinds of people who catch his attention, and how he will nurture his followers. These passages illustrate Matthew's special interest in presenting Jesus as a source of blessing and comfort to a weary world.

Matthew 5:1-12

(Blessed Are...)

One of the first things Jesus says out loud in Matthew, for a gathering of people to hear, is the word *blessed*. He's not speaking about the quality of his own life. He promises blessings for others. The promises would probably surprise most people, because Jesus's promises don't square with common expectations. No wonder crowds follow him, eager to hear what he proposes.

One of the first things Jesus says out loud in Matthew, for a gathering of people to hear, is the word *blessed*.

First, we should recognize that a lot happens in Matthew before we receive *any* up-close view of Jesus making promises to a group. The Gospel covers much ground over its first two chapters, starting with Jesus's birth, the visit of the magi from the East, and his family's flight to Egypt to escape a murderous tyrant. The narrative stays fast-paced in its next two chapters, telling us about Jesus's baptism, his encounters with the devil in the desert, and four of the first people who choose to follow him. At last Jesus starts ministering in public, preaching "the good news" about God's "kingdom" and healing people (4:23-25). His popularity quickly spreads widely: throughout Syria, Galilee, the

Decapolis (east of the Jordan River), Jerusalem, Judea, and further beyond the Jordan. That didn't take long.

Precisely at this point, with Jesus already drawing crowds, Matthew gives us a rich taste of what makes Jesus appealing. The first big public event that this Gospel narrates, starting in Matthew 5, is a sermon commonly called "The Sermon on the Mount." Jesus's "sermons," or extended speeches, in Matthew appear to be literary creations. To help the Gospel's audiences understand Jesus's significance, some of his teachings were arranged together and are presented as single events. They play a part in shaping Matthew's distinctive perspective and structure. The timing of this first sermon, at the outset of Jesus's ministry, sends a signal about the importance Matthew attaches to Jesus's influence as a teacher.

By contrast, in the Gospel according to Mark the first extended public scene in Jesus's ministry is an exorcism of an unclean spirit. That's on-brand for Mark, which calls attention to Jesus's authority to wage an urgent, cosmic conflict against spiritual powers. The first big story of public ministry in Luke describes Jesus as he reads from Isaiah in a synagogue and announces he fulfills the ancient prophet's grand vision of liberation. That fits Luke's accent on the prophetic aspects of Jesus's life. In John, the inaugural scene—turning water into wine at a wedding—provides a miraculous demonstration of surplus, surprise, and symbolism. Additional signs come later in John. In Matthew, a sermon, Jesus's opening statement, tells us Jesus is a teacher. Matthew lays it down: Jesus has something to say. He begins with blessings.

The sermon bursts in with poetry. There's a rhythm to the first nine sentences, which all begin, "Blessed are ..." It's a rhythm carried by promises, not accusations. These are declarations, not commands. They promise relief, not tests. Jesus expresses grace in its purest form, gifts with no strings attached.

Who's blessed? Jesus names eight different groups of people. (His ninth "Blessed are ..." sentence is about the same group as his eighth one, folks who suffer religiously motivated persecution.) He doesn't define the eight categories; they open our imaginations. All eight share something in common, however: they are the types of people who often find it difficult to keep their heads above water in Jesus's world, as well as in our own.

Generally speaking, people in the Roman-controlled Mediterranean region during the first century lived in an agonistic society. The word *agonistic* comes from the Greek word *agōn*, which means "struggle" or "contest." It's also behind the word *agony*. An agonistic society is one marked by competition. It doesn't mean that everyone is your enemy. Rather, in that kind of culture, social status, power, and privilege matter in every social interaction. You know your place in the pecking order, and you might lose your advantages if you don't guard them. Never give rivals a chance to best you. It's not such a foreign concept, is it? There are agonistic elements in our modern democratic and capitalistic societies. Sometimes a sense of struggle fuels progress. Sometimes it crushes people.

Other places were more agonistic than Galilee, where Jesus lived, but he and his neighbors knew how things worked. In that kind of culture, the people Jesus promises to bless at the beginning of his first sermon are the ones who tend to bring up the rear in the rat race, because in a competitive world they're the easiest to step over, take advantage of, overpower, or just ignore. Whom does he have in mind?

The poor in spirit? They are people whose vitality has been broken or taken from them, making it difficult for them to hope anymore or to have a sense of their own self-worth.

Those who mourn? All of us must go through seasons of mourning, but I propose that Jesus means people who never find their way amid the loss and emptiness that grief creates. These are people who must live without parts of themselves, perhaps through the bitter and irretrievable loss of a spouse, a child, a job, a community, innocence, or health.

Those who are meek? This isn't about shyness or politeness. Picture the people who get stepped on and whose voices are never heard. These are our neighbors who have no advocates or who just can't get their foot into a door of opportunity without it being slammed on them.

Those who hunger and thirst for righteousness? Jesus refers to people who get cheated or unfairly blamed. Understand "righteousness" here as justice. To hunger for it is to long to have the truth told. In our predatory world, systems and prejudices deny justice to many people; the systems are designed that way.

Those who are merciful? At least a little mercy is a good thing for everyone to give. I won't hate you for causing a fender bender. But if I'm too merciful and generous, won't that make me a sucker and a target for scams? In a dog-eat-dog world, the merciful dog might end up as someone else's lunch.

Those who are pure in heart? We all should strive for purity, right? Of course. But I suppose most of us have lowered our standards for ourselves and the world so we can avoid being disappointed. We've learned to tolerate corruption. We overlook the injustices around us, chalking them up to the cost of doing business or achieving a greater good. True and uncompromising purity in heart can leave someone stuck with constant heartache as they navigate a mean and power-obsessed world.

Peacemakers? Jesus doesn't mean the times I signed petitions and wrote letters to my senators. Jesus singles out people willing to place themselves in the midst of conflict, whether it's on a battlefield, in a neighborhood, in a conference room, or around a dining-room table. Think of people who get involved so they can foster reconciliation. Think of people who put reputations or careers on the line to help others. Think of people who provide sanctuary to those who need it.

Those who are persecuted? Jesus specifically indicates persecution because of someone's commitment to God's righteousness and someone's affiliation with Jesus. He doesn't say that suffering is a good or redemptive thing, just that aligning oneself with him may earn a person some enemies. He acknowledges his message is going

5

to upset the status quo, if that hasn't already been made clear in the sermon so far.

Jesus's overarching message goes out to people who are vulnerable, people who are generally disadvantaged in a world that rewards advantages, people who are dissatisfied with the way things are, and people who suffer because of their convictions. All of them are now, or are about to be, blessed.

Personally, I have a hard time getting too excited about the English word *blessed*. It typically gets used in saccharine or sanctimonious ways. Other times people use it as a synonym for cheerful or fortunate. The Greek word that we translate "blessed" carries a sense of being "happy," but not in a smiley or delighted sense. When we consider that word as it's used in other relevant literature, such as Greek translations of the Old Testament, its meaning is closer to "satisfied" or "unburdened"—perhaps the way you feel when someone has done you a favor, honored your dignity, or given you a valuable gift. Jesus, therefore, promises revitalizing *contentedness* to a range of people who need it, declaring them recipients of something useful, refreshing, and life-giving.

What makes this surprising? People who grieve or suffer religious persecution don't usually see gifts coming their direction. Jesus launches his ministry by inverting our assumptions. People in his audience surely must think he's got it backwards. Aren't the strong and self-assured people the blessed ones? No. Jesus has a different reality in mind. Changes are coming for precisely the kinds of people whose lives seem far, far from "unburdened" or relieved.

When Jesus calls those people blessed, he announces his determination to being among them and making a difference in their lives. These verses function as a mission statement for his entire ministry. He discloses where we should expect to find him: among the people who live beleaguered and hard-luck lives. Begin your search for him and his influence there.

We misunderstand Jesus's words if we take "blessed are" to mean "cheer up" or "recognize that you're really the fortunate ones." Jesus isn't insisting that the people who customarily get treated like objects or who find life difficult are somehow surprisingly happier than comfortable people. He's not saying that simpler lives make for better life. He's not suggesting that pain is good for you. Instead, he's declaring that people who have been denied peace and satisfaction will find it, through him. Jesus promises to embrace the unembraced. That's the blessing.

Through his embrace, Jesus subverts conventional notions about what it means to be successful or content.

Through his embrace, Jesus subverts conventional notions about what it means to be successful or content. If we're going to understand what he's up to, we're going to have to change our systems of measurement and our values. A new society is coming into being, Jesus promises. It's not beginning among people who enjoy the success, belonging, respect, self-reliance, and prosperity that take so much of our energy to hold on to and defend.

Matthew 6:30-33

(Promises for Those of Little Faith)

In the second half of the Sermon on the Mount, we discover how Jesus acknowledges human frailty and understands the difficulties that come with trying to trust God. Probably because I occasionally talk to my plants to encourage them, I compare Jesus to a careful gardener. He knows a seedling is vulnerable, yet he can perceive its potential to grow into something majestic. Jesus understands that faith often requires delicate handling for it to blossom.

Jesus reassures people "of little faith" that God is reliable and is concerned about their needs. He uses the expression *you of little faith* gently, not to scold. I think he's talking about all of us, or at least most of us. Having a limited amount of faith isn't a fault as much as it's simply part of what it means to be human in a world that often tells us we have to fight tooth and nail to secure our own future. Leave the anxious striving to other people, Jesus says, it's what "the gentiles" do. (He means the people who don't know God's trustworthiness.)

Faith doesn't automatically burst into being as something sturdy. It needs to be nurtured. Good thing Jesus is a nurturer. This is a crucial theme in Matthew.

The English nouns *faith*, *belief*, and *trust* are all legitimate translations of the same Greek word. I think *trust* best gets at what Jesus is talking about: people with "little trust." Bible translations usually opt for the word *faith*, but the idea usually isn't about "believing in God," as if it's some decision we make with our minds. Instead, biblical "faith" is about trusting God—trusting that what God says about us is true and trusting that God's ways are good for us and for our neighbors. Jesus's emphasis is less cognitive and more experiential: how does a person of "faith" actually live?

With the expression *little faith* Jesus acknowledges that we're still growing and learning. Trust takes time in any relationship. Jesus says he's okay with that. He will take care of people with little faith. He repeats the expression in 8:23-27, when he protects his followers during a violent storm as they sail across the Sea of Galilee (see also 14:28-33). Versions of the expression appear also in 16:8 and 17:20, and just once elsewhere in the whole New Testament (Luke 12:28). Matthew seems to like using it.

Returning to the Sermon on the Mount in Matthew 6, we also find there a promise Jesus makes to us, to anyone of little faith. He urges his listeners to seek God's kingdom first, then "all these things"—the basic necessities of life—"will be given to you as well" (v. 33). He doesn't seem to be pledging to provide food, clothing, and housing with a miraculous wave of the hand. He promises that God's desired society—the emerging kingdom of heaven—will make our worrying obsolete. As God's ways come to pass, we know how to use God's gifts to ensure that everyone receives care. That's a promise, one that we can begin to realize now if we let God nourish our meager ability to trust. It helps when we practice that together.

Matthew 20:1-16

(Workers in the Vineyard)

No passage in Matthew illustrates how outrageous, lavish, and upending God's grace is better than this parable does. It captures the magnitude of generosity embedded in God's desire to bless the world through Jesus Christ and the Kingdom he inaugurates.

Jesus lived and taught in an agricultural economy where most manual laborers worked land owned by other people. The parable, therefore, begins with a scenario that would be very familiar. The man who owns a vineyard hires workers at the start of the day and offers to pay them fairly; one denarius for a day's work was standard. A few hours later he enlists more people and is less specific about the wages but promises to pay "whatever is right" (literally, "whatever is just"). He says the same thing to people again at noon and 3:00.

Near the end of the day, one hour before quitting time, he finds potential workers standing around. They explain, "No one has hired us," but he sends them to the vineyard anyway. We should pause here and consider who these people might be. Nothing suggests laziness. They've been waiting all day to work. I suppose I could be one of them. I'm not especially strong and my back can't take much strain. I'm better at drinking the fruit of the vine than I am at cultivating grapes. So we're probably talking about people who are infirm or who are getting on in years who remain unhired at 5:00. Maybe some of them have bad reputations in the village and aren't considered trustworthy. Others might not speak the local language. Someone might be coughing too much or look like a life of poverty has robbed them of their productivity. In other words, the vineyard owner hires the people who struggle to find work and who most need sources of income. What will they receive when he pays "whatever is right"?

We learn the answer right away: everyone gets a denarius, the amount for a full day's work. It doesn't matter if you worked one hour, three hours, six hours, or the whole day; to the landowner, each person receives precisely what he thinks is right or just. We don't hear how the 5:00 crowd responds, but I'm sure they're elated. They aren't paid according to how much they produced but according to what they and presumably their families need to survive another day. The landowner holds nothing against them, not their disadvantages, their misfortune, their stigmas, or their bad choices.

The people who worked all day are understandably upset. They expect more, because that's the way the game is supposed to work. Even if the landowner wants to be generous, why not show great generosity to all? Don't the most able still deserve the most reward? Didn't they contribute more? Wouldn't the vineyard benefit more from the full day's effort they put into it? They complain that the landowner, by paying all the other workers the same wage, has "made them" (the latecomers), "equal to us." Their effectiveness and their virtue haven't received proper recognition.

Jesus doesn't imply that the full-day workers were fooled or cheated. For them, the system worked as it was supposed to. The crux of the parable emerges when those workers respond with jealousy toward the landowner's generosity. The landowner recognizes that the late-day workers couldn't make a living in the normal system, so he delivers them from the system and dignifies them with what they need. He desires a system that works for them instead.

Jesus isn't giving lessons in how to run a business. If the landowner starts to behave this way every day, no workers will ever show up at his vineyard again before late afternoon. Nor should we limit the parable to mean that empowering people is solely a matter of making them the object of financial charity. Take the symbolism of monetary wages as suggestive and partial, not a comprehensive depiction of how dignity is recognized or bestowed. The parable's primary effect is to illustrate how God's generosity benefits those who need it most. Remember how Jesus announced in his first sermon that he's more interested in blessing people who are poor in spirit and meek than he is in awarding extra points to folks who have healthy self-esteem and possess all they need to make everything work in their favor? This parable offers a similar promise, and it shows what a bad look it is when people cry "foul" in response to God's partiality toward those who most need blessing.

Jesus begins the parable by announcing that it illustrates an aspect of God's kingdom. When it comes to the wholeness God offers, God is determined not to leave anyone out. No one is disqualified because they don't have the right résumé. Blessings aren't parceled out according to what people have earned, but according to what's required to elevate anyone within the Kingdom's reach. The landowner seems to delight in the fact that he's a little unfair, as the world measures fairness with balance sheets and scales. A generous God makes sure that blessings flow. Period. That's the promise Jesus makes, and it's one he acts out over and over in his ministry.

Matthew 25:31-46
(Sheep and Goats)

We started this chapter where Jesus begins, with the opening lines of the Sermon on the Mount. At the other end of his public ministry, he makes some more astonishing promises. Just before the plot against his life begins, the plot that will result in his crucifixion, Jesus offers one last extended sermon. He teaches nonstop in Matthew 24–25, mostly offering parables about the culmination of all things and the eventual fullness of the kingdom of heaven. The last of those parables, his final public statement in Matthew before the story of his ministry turns into the story of his death, is about a group of sheep that encounters Jesus without knowing it. Like the parable of the workers in the vineyard, this one appears only in Matthew.

The parable offers a vision of the future. It occurs when Jesus, "the Son of Man," rules over all creation in glory. Jesus, the king, gathers the nations for judgment. He tells us that he sorts the nations into two groups, one identified as sheep and one as goats. The animals, of course, represent groups of people; this is theology, not zoology. The sheep "inherit the kingdom," but the goats are sent to punishment. As morality tales go, this one looks pretty simplistic on the surface: there are two groups going in two very different directions, with no apparent middle ground.

How does the king separate the sheep and the goats? I always assumed that it's an easy job. Since I grew up in the suburbs, all I knew about livestock I learned from picture books and cartoons, in which sheep are fluffy and rounder, while goats have beards and eat everything in sight. I had to go to graduate school before I learned that undomesticated sheep and goats in Jesus's time were nearly indistinguishable to most people. They looked almost the same. Only someone with a trained eye could do the sorting.

In other words, there's no obvious difference between the people arrayed before the king. Virtually no one can tell from glancing at them who's kind and who's mean, who's educated and who isn't, which ones use iPhones and who has an Android. The sheep and goats are mixed together. The king needs some kind of experienced insights to tell them apart.

We learn about those insights when Jesus praises the sheep for giving him food and drink when he was hungry and thirsty. They welcomed him when he was an outsider. They clothed him when he was naked, offered care when he was ill, and visited him in prison to supply and encourage him. In short, they opened their hearts, homes, and generosity to him when he found himself in need. On the other side, the goats all failed to offer the same care to Jesus in those same circumstances.

Here's a vital detail in the story: both groups are surprised by what Jesus says. Sheep and goats alike say, in essence, "What are you talking about? We never saw you. We never gave you aid. Where were you in all of that?"

Jesus explains himself. In the process he also reveals himself. He opens the parable, saying that when people go out of their way to demonstrate compassion to someone who really needs it (or when they fail to do so) they meet (or ignore) Jesus himself. Jesus announces that he can be encountered in "one of the least of these." He doesn't explain what he means by that expression, but the context of the parable implies that he's talking about anyone who needs help because they lack basic needs of food, water, shelter, clothing, community, and justice.

Jesus tells us where we can find him: within those who endure desperate conditions.

Again, Jesus tells us where we can find him: within those who endure desperate conditions. We can say, therefore, that there's something sacramental about the acts of kindness that the sheep perform. In Christian tradition, sacraments are ways we encounter divine grace in materials that otherwise seem ordinary. The specific details remain mysterious, but somehow we encounter Jesus Christ through the water of baptism and through the bread and wine of the Lord's Supper. (Some Christian denominations consider there to be additional sacraments too.) Jesus says that concrete acts of love, decency, and acknowledging someone else's human dignity also create opportunities for encountering him. We might not call those good deeds one of *the* sacraments, but the sheep's actions are sacramental insofar as they bring us into Christ's presence.

The point isn't that compassion and generosity are ways of acting like Jesus, although they are. Rather, Jesus focuses attention on where he is, or who he is. To encounter Jesus we don't need to find a special shrine or take a pilgrimage to the Sea of Galilee. He presents himself to us in our neighbors who need a hand, no matter how they got into that condition. The people who show mercy are the ones Jesus calls "righteous."

We ought to recall that the parable also includes people—symbolized as goats—who neglect Jesus and receive "eternal fire" and "eternal punishment." It's frightening imagery, and I wish it wasn't part of the story. The imagery, however, appears not only here but also in other parts of Matthew. We'll explore it in more detail later, in chapter 2. For now, let's simply notice that Jesus's harsh response to the goats appears not to be retaliation because of how he was neglected. The problem is that "the least of these" in the world were left hungry, naked, and vulnerable. That appears to trigger a particular vengeance, which we will revisit in due time.

Many congregations gravitate to this parable to declare that acts of compassion are essential parts of Christian faith. The parable spurs those believers to pursue a just society and to remember Jesus's own commitment of solidarity to those who dwell in the most neglected or exploited corners of society. In my Presbyterian denomination, some congregations even take a pledge to be a "Matthew 25 church" and prioritize ministries of social justice.

I'm all for mobilizing congregations to make a difference in the world, but I also want to point out that the parable is about much more than motivating a congregation's mission. The parable isn't primarily about church people and how they should prioritize mercy. Instead, it's a story about "the nations," which in Matthew's perspective means the people who are more or less "out there." It's about the wider world. The word *nations* translates the Greek word *ethnos*, which also gives us words like ethnicity. Jesus isn't talking about "nations" as geopolitical units; he's talking about the wide range of peoples in the world, with all their cultural variety. The parable is therefore answering an implicit question: what about the rest of the world, people who don't live near Galilee and don't have opportunity to know Jesus? Can even they come to experience his blessings?

The parable answers emphatically, Yes. Jesus is accessible to anyone. In his presence within "the least of these," all people have opportunity to encounter the love of God. Jesus opens the door very wide here, saying that his blessings aren't limited to a group of insiders. His promises don't belong to the church alone, not even to Christians alone.

I should be clear: I'm not saying that everyone who eases the burdens of someone who suffers is really a Christian without knowing it. I'm not suggesting that no other religious tradition has validity. I don't want to restrict God and narrowly define the ways people encounter God. Those matters are God's to determine, not mine.

I do believe, however, that the parable makes key promises that should expand our imagination for what's going on with Jesus. One is that people who show mercy are people who imitate divine righteousness. Mercy matters in Matthew, much more so than correct doctrines. A second promise is that God doesn't limit the people who can have access to experiencing divine goodness. That experience isn't based on who prays the most or who donates the most money or who spends their time writing books about the Bible. The experience comes to people who encounter God's love in the warmth they show to their neighbor—for the sake of that neighbor's dignity and well-being. This parable offers an important reminder that Jesus hasn't left the world or stopped showing up since the Resurrection. He's here. He's outside the door. We in the church don't get to control where and how God becomes present to other people. And we certainly don't get to be the ones who decide whose faith is valid and whose is not.

When it comes to determining the authenticity of someone's faith, Jesus is better clued in than we are.

15

Reflections

Where should someone begin an exploration of Matthew's Gospel? Instead of starting with the virgin birth, Jesus's baptism, the Crucifixion, or the Resurrection, I choose to begin with the promises Jesus makes and the people to whom he promises them. These passages provide a glimpse into the "kingdom of heaven" that Jesus so eagerly announces. He imagines the possibility of a new society in which no one is denied their dignity and wholeness. As we will see, Jesus manifests his vision for a renewed humanity in a variety of ways. His ministry involves more than compassion alone. He'll also bring his followers along to share his work and will spend time—too much time, according to his opponents—hanging out with disreputable people like "tax collectors and sinners" (9:10-13).

You might suspect I've started with Matthew's most generous stories because I want to set Jesus in the most positive light possible. It's true that there are passages in this Gospel that portray him in more alarming ways, as agitated and promising punishment. We'll look at some of those soon enough. My reason for beginning here, with a peek into the depths of divine grace and the kinds of people to whom Jesus is eager to show his grace, is to orient us to the fervent passion that propels Jesus forward in Matthew. His overriding desire to protect and restore vulnerable or disregarded people expresses itself at the beginning of his public ministry. Likewise, he remains present among those folks, eager to be encountered, at his ministry's conclusion. The two stories that bookend his ministry, along with others that fall in between, reveal his intentions. Those intentions direct how we should read the whole story. Jesus's declarations of grace give us our bearings. We can't forget them. Now that you've read this first chapter you'll need to keep what it says in mind as you journey through the next five.

Understanding the blessings and comfort Jesus promises will help us understand the anger and punishment he threatens. The enormity of Jesus's concern for overmatched people is equal to the intensity of his frustration with the people and powers that oppress and threaten them. When the abusive and negligent people are religious people, folks who claim to align themselves with God's desires, he gets especially upset.

Understanding the blessings and comfort Jesus promises will help us understand the anger and punishment he threatens.

We church people sometimes fall into the trap of romanticizing Jesus, imagining him as if every conscientious person who met him would have joined his movement. We forget that the Gospels portray his message as divisive. We err if we assume Jesus's ministry was mostly about encouragement, as if he comes to a world that just needs a pep talk or a hug. Rather, he comes thinking that the world needs to be remade and its norms redefined. He promises that God, through him, will be the one to set it all on a new path. His assessment of what the world needs isn't at all limited to the first-century culture in which he lived. It applies still today. Matthew urges us to continue learning what it means to long for divine blessing and comfort to reach completion. That requires all of us to kindle one another's flickering trust that God is reliable to make it happen.

Chapter 2

Promised Judgment

Passages to Explore:

Matthew 3:1-12   (John the Baptist)
Matthew 7:24-27   (Two Houses)
Matthew 13:47-50   (The Dragnet)

It's difficult to talk about divine judgment.

I regularly meet people with horrible stories about the pain they carry from their experiences in congregations that used the Bible as a weapon to terrorize or shame them.

Moreover, a common reason people cite for staying away from churches and opportunities for Christian worship is the judgmentalism they perceive among Christians. Too many believers think their faith grants them a license to decide exactly what's sinful. They determine which specific sins deserve public condemnation and which people should be singled out for criticism over who they are and what they do. To distance ourselves from those gross displays of hypocrisy and intolerance, many of us gravitate toward biblical passages that describe

God's love and acceptance while steering around those that describe a coming judgment.

Matthew's depiction of Jesus nevertheless presses us to try to hold both kinds of passages together. They aren't contradictory, but understanding why they appear together in Jesus's teachings requires a closer look.

Recall what I wrote in this book's Introduction about Matthew's emphasis on judgment and punishment. As we dig into this topic, one thing we'll notice is a pronounced dualism. Dualism divides the world into two mutually exclusive camps. We experienced that in the previous chapter when we examined the parable about arranging the nations into groups of sheep and goats. In a dualistic perspective, a person must be either one or the other, and each person is utterly defined as such. In such a worldview, you can't like both cats and dogs; you're either entirely a cat person or entirely a dog person. More seriously, the dualism in Matthew recognizes only "the children of the kingdom" and "the children of the evil one" (13:38). The rewarded and the punished. Winners and losers.

Taken the wrong way and extended too far, dualism easily becomes a recipe for Christian judgmentalism. Once you're convinced the world contains only clear sinners and clear saints, you're prone to start trying to determine who belongs in which camp.

If you're a fan of the comic strip *The Far Side*, maybe you remember the one where people are lined up to enter heaven and hell. The panel is split, showing the line into heaven on top (of course it's on the top) filled with people wearing wings and standing on a cloud. The line into hell appears on the bottom, with people in a cave whose floor is on fire. On top, an angel hands a harp to each person, saying, "Welcome to heaven…Here's your harp." On the bottom a demon hands out accordions, saying, "Welcome to hell…Here's your accordion." It's an example of how popular depictions about heaven and hell have sprung forth from the dualistic categories that confront us in many Gospel stories. Those depictions distort our impressions of God's judgment as if it's only about being placed on a road to a specific, eternal destination—one with pure bliss and the other with pure pain. It's as if a person takes either the up escalator or the down escalator and thus concludes the judgment for all time.

I urge my students to reevaluate what they assume when they think about God's judgment. Viewing it as the occasion when souls are weighed in scales before being funneled into one of two separate, final, never-ending destinations isn't accurate. Nor is it a gathering where everyone watches video of each time you sneaked office supplies home from work. Nor does Jesus present it as his opportunity to dish out a measured punishment for each and every sin. That's what mob bosses do, not God.

I admit the Bible contains some individual passages that might support those ideas, such as Daniel 12:2. The most harmful theological proposals tend to be the ones constructed from a single biblical passage. The wider witness of Scripture compels us to embrace more nuance, especially when it comes to interpreting the Bible's dualistic imagery.

The symbolism used when Matthew focuses on God's judgment mostly describes a time when the true nature of a thing will be revealed; it's a time when things are sorted based on what they truly are.

The symbolism used when Matthew focuses on God's judgment mostly describes a time when the true nature of a thing will be revealed; it's a time when things are sorted based on what they truly are. Likewise, Jesus's teachings mention future rewards and punishments, incentivizing certain behaviors. But we should be wary about carrying the dualism too far, as if it can accurately and fully capture either the human condition (the blessed vs. the cursed) or the idea that judgment is a threshold to receiving one's just deserts (eternal pleasure vs. eternal pain). Jesus promises that God will judge, but that isn't equivalent to promising that God will send certain people to hell for eternity.

As we will see, Matthew's references to judgment begin with promises about God's commitment to reveal the truth, expose injustices, and transform the world. Any exploration of divine judgment should likewise begin there.

Matthew 3:1-12

(John the Baptist)

It's tough to know what to do with John the Baptist. Let's be honest: he's weird. He wouldn't make it past the first interview if your congregation was calling a new pastor. More to the point of our study, he also preaches messages that appear difficult to square with everything Jesus represents. John speaks about wrath and introduces Jesus as a "more powerful" figure who will collect valuable wheat and incinerate useless chaff. Jesus preaches very different things, as we have seen, when he begins his public ministry.

John and his hair-raising preaching are vital, however, for setting Matthew's tone. John insists that something needs to be fixed. John's appearance tells us the story about Jesus that follows will be about repairing a broken world. John's teachings promise a repair process that involves, at least at first, sorting out what (or who) is working as it should and what (or who) is troublesome. I do similar things when I try to weed a flowerbed or clean out my neglected fridge when I start smelling something suspicious.

Matthew's way of describing John evokes memories of the prophet Elijah, whom the Bible says lived over 800 years earlier. John's physical appearance resembles Elijah's (see 2 Kings 1:8). Jesus in Matthew 11:14 identifies John as a kind of remanifestation of Elijah (see Malachi 4:5-6). What tone do memories of Elijah set for Matthew? God is about to reveal the truth of things, and people will have choices to make. After all, Elijah is best remembered for calling everyone to choose between their idolatry and the God of Israel (1 Kings 18:21). Elijah also envisioned the start of a repair process, but his methods were more severe and, frankly, more hands-on than John's, because he executed 450 false prophets (1 Kings 18:17-40). The harsh words John directs to Pharisees and Sadducees—who were religious leaders among John's fellow Jews—look rather tame by comparison.

John's baptism was a ritual involving repentance and confession. He sees those responses as essential for what's coming: "Repent, for the kingdom of heaven has come near" (3:2). Jesus says the exact same thing later, when he starts preaching after John's arrest (4:17). Although later in Matthew we learn that Jesus isn't precisely the kind of God-appointed figure that John expects (3:14; 11:2-3), nevertheless John's and Jesus's messages rhyme.

Don't assume that repentance and confession are simply the same as expressing contrition and remorse. (Feeling sad about our wrongdoings isn't usually the first step. If you're a parent perhaps you've tried the ineffective tactic of instructing your child, "Tell your cousin you feel bad about eating both of the ice-cream sandwiches I left in the freezer for you two.") Repentance and confession are first and foremost about truth-telling. Sorrow might come later. By "truth-telling," I mean admission; we admit our wrongs. In doing so, we may also lay bare our brokenness. By using "we" and "our," I'm calling attention to our communal wrongs and faults, not just our personal ones. We tell the truth about our world, our society, our neighborhood, our congregation, our family, and ourselves. Telling, hearing, and acknowledging the truth is essential for repair.

The most interesting aspect of this passage shows itself when the religious leaders arrive. John gets chippy. He doesn't assail Pharisees and Sadducees because they are *Jews*, as if they somehow represent Judaism as a whole. John isn't imagining a new religion starting with the arrival of Jesus. Nor does John consider Judaism as something defective. John directs his most dire words to that group because they are *religious leaders*. As such, they have tremendous influence over how everyone else lives out their religious commitments.

In chapter 5 we'll spend more time with Matthew's depiction of Pharisees. For now, let's note the power any religious leaders possess. They can make faithful people stingy toward their neighbors. They can rob religious devotion of its joy. As we'll see in future chapters, Matthew doesn't want us to miss the idea that Jesus disdains religious apathy. Hypocrisy sets his teeth on edge, especially when leaders are the culprits. Remember last chapter's discussions of people with "little faith" and those who are "poor in spirit"? Jesus won't allow other people to make religion into a burden for folks like them.

When teaching the Gospels to my students, most of whom are preparing to lead Christian communities, I have to press home two points whenever we talk about Jesus's hostility toward religious hypocrisy. First, most of us in the classroom (and maybe most reading this book) resemble the Pharisees more than any other people in the Gospels. (The Sadducees, who were priestly elites, are a different story. Usually no one in a seminary classroom is as wealthy or powerful as they were!) We all want to align with the disciples, Mary Magdalene, or the Prodigal Son. Instead, like the Pharisees and other leaders, my students (and I) have certain spiritual traditions and values we seek to uphold. We put significant effort into strengthening religious institutions and communities. Those aren't bad things, but they can make us suspicious of other people whose ideas (like Jesus's) differ from what we're used to. We get defensive when we're criticized. John's and Jesus's criticisms of Jewish religious leaders aren't attempts to tear down Judaism. The opposite is closer to the truth. Jesus and John are trying to reform a particular religious imagination that they think has grown stale and may have consigned some people to outside the house looking in. We shouldn't presume we're safe from doing the same.

The second thing I emphasize is that John and Jesus aren't targeting religion in general, as if they're offering a new way of connecting with God that's totally unconcerned with history, rituals, leadership structures, doctrine, and community. The problem isn't religion or even religious people. Rather, a problem that really piques John and Jesus is when religious insiders—and even people who claim they're not "religious"—cause or become complicit in the suffering of others.

John, therefore, foresees a reckoning, an appraisal. Maybe he *longs* for it too. John talks the way people talk when they're out of patience and have grown utterly sick of injustice and wickedness. People like that have calculated the cost of oppression, as costs get measured by human misery, social decay, and environmental ruin. That's the urgent tone John sets. He urges everyone to face the truth about themselves and the world, because that truth will soon be made plain. The truth entails learning the consequences of our transgressions. It's also discovering the good that results from our merciful acts. Don't despair, for John offers a path to forgiveness too. Don't skip too quickly over that part. Even when John preaches to religious leaders, he does more than hurl warnings; he also issues invitations. He calls people to align themselves with "the one who is coming" after him.

Jesus takes things forward from here. For when the truth does get told, someone has to do something about it.

Matthew 7:24-27

(Two Houses)

In the previous chapter we explored the opening lines of Jesus's Sermon on the Mount. Now we look at its ending. (In chapter 3 we'll return to examine yet more of it!) The sermon's final verses conclude a section (7:13-27) in which Jesus compares two gates to walk through, one leading to life and one to destruction. Then he describes two kinds of trees, one bearing good fruit and one bad. Next are the people who call him "Lord" and recognize the power of his name, but some of them remain unknown by him. Finally, he contrasts a person who builds a house on a rock with someone who builds a house on sand. Only the former house survives when rain, floods, and wind arrive.

The first housebuilder is wise, while the second is foolish. The wise one acts on Jesus's words, but the foolish one ignores his truths.

The wise one acts on Jesus's words, but the foolish one ignores his truths.

I wasn't kidding earlier when I warned you to get ready for a lot of dualism. Jesus describes just two kinds of existence or two kinds of responses. He doesn't consider whether a third house, one built on semi-stable land, might suffer only partial damage in a storm, or whether a person might act on Jesus's words some days while failing to do so on others. Jesus keeps the differences absolute. One or the other. He might do this because he's a good preacher, and he's trying to motivate his hearers (and us, the readers) to remember that it's not too late. He's not describing your inalterable future; he's offering you another chance. The dualism's main job is to lay a choice before you in the starkest of terms.

Jesus clearly knows his Bible. Actually, there was no clear-cut, defined Jewish "Bible" when he lived, but there were widely revered, sacred Jewish writings in circulation that eventually found their way into a formal "Bible." He clearly knows the Law (which became the first five books in Jews' and Christians' Bibles), the Prophets (a collection of books that would eventually constitute a large segment of the Bible), the Psalms, and perhaps other texts. Those scriptures, as well as other ancient writings, frequently employ a teaching device known as the "two ways." For example:

> *"I call heaven and earth to witness against you today that I have set before you life and death, blessings and curses. Choose life so that you and your descendants may live."*
>
> *(Deuteronomy 30:19)*

Thus says the LORD: See, I am setting before you the way of life and the way of death.

(Jeremiah 21:8)

The LORD watches over the way of the righteous,
but the way of the wicked will perish.

(Psalm 1:6)

Jesus and other ancient teachers weren't naïve. They understood the complexities of life and the ambiguity of moral judgments. Instructing people about "two ways" doesn't insist that life is simple or that true virtue requires perfection. The power of the "two ways" motif lies, rather, in how it urges people to align themselves with God and to trust God's ways of describing the world, justice, and human flourishing.

Ask a preacher and I think they'll confirm that one of the most difficult things about preaching is knowing how much to say and how much to leave for another day. The rough draft of any preacher's next sermon ought to have questions scribbled all over the margins: *Is my main message clear in this paragraph? Is this a place to introduce more nuance, or should I keep it simpler? Will they remember God forgives them, or should I emphasize that again?* Jesus evidently decides to make a single, bold point in these verses using a series of related metaphors. The magnitude of the moment calls for forcefulness instead of a full-blown explanation. So Jesus lets it fly in his inaugural sermon: *I'm determined to get your attention. Something's very wrong. There are many bad choices in front of you. I've come to fix things. Don't miss your chance.*

At this early stage in Jesus's preaching career, it's about urgency. He therefore preaches urgently. Nuance will have to wait. We go beyond the basic intention of this passage if we take his words about two kinds of houses (really, two kinds of builders) as license for dividing the world into insiders and outsiders, or the saved and the damned. As if we know! As if that's our decision to make! As if those categories are all there are. A "two ways" mindset tends to mislead us if we extend it too far and let it reduce our outlook on the world to something too simple.

At the same time, Jesus clearly means business. He hasn't come to tell everyone that everything's just fine the way it is. As we've discussed, he comes to warn, because the need for course-correction and renewal is so real. He also comes to invite, because he longs for people to experience the better way he offers.

We also distort this passage if we turn its imagery into a warning about a final judgment, in which a house standing or falling says something about what ultimately happens to someone after this life. Rather, Jesus is talking about how a person (or a community) should build so their life and character can withstand whatever metaphorical storms may test one's integrity or foundations. The passage is still about judgment, technically speaking, insofar as it promises that truths about us will be revealed, specifically the truth about our lives' foundations. Not all judgment is final judgment. Sometimes people get chances to rebuild homes once the storms pass and we realize our errors or weaknesses.

As I've mentioned, Jesus sees the world as woefully in need of repair, and part of the problem is that people hunger after the wrong things. Destructive things. The imagery of his sermon asks us to take stock. We make economic and moral choices that lead to ruin for ourselves and others. We let ourselves become enticed by false promises about what makes for a good life or who deserves justice. We find religious devotion empowering, but we ignore the humility and open-heartedness that Jesus models.

Jesus never says the solution is trying harder until you ace the exam. The solution lies in anchoring oneself to the security of his word, trusting the good news he enacts in his teachings and deeds.

Matthew 13:47-50

(The Dragnet)

In Matthew (as in Luke) a large percentage of Jesus's teachings comes in the form of parables. He often says they reveal something about the kingdom of heaven. Other ancient teachers and writers also composed parables to make their points. They're effective teaching tools because they can jolt us into considering an idea from a new perspective. If you had an English teacher introduce you to different types of "figurative language" in school, now's the time to awaken those memories. The English word *parable* comes from the Greek *parabolē*, which literally means something placed alongside something else. Jesus gives us a peak into the Kingdom he's inaugurating by telling us what it's like. "Look at it this way, in comparison to this other thing, and you'll see something new," Jesus essentially says.

He does not say, "The Kingdom is exactly the same as this other thing." Rather, he illuminates a particular aspect of the Kingdom, as we've seen already with parables about paying workers who toil for various numbers of hours and about separating sheep from goats. The stories he tells usually describe activities that people in an agrarian society would find familiar, such as planting seeds, finding a lost sheep, and, in this case, catching fish.

As short stories go, this one about a massive dragnet placed into the sea and pulled ashore is not too exciting. It's extremely short and rather non-suspenseful, focused not so much on a compelling plot but an activity: sorting sea creatures.

I say "sea creatures" and not "fish," because Jesus doesn't specify fish. Translators supply that word because that's usually what you're hoping to find in a full net. Jesus's language says, in effect, that the net will "gather together" all sorts of things; he says "each kind" or "each category." In other words, there will presumably be valuable fish in there, but other kinds of critters, too, things that commercial fishers don't want. Dragnets bring everything together. As for the creatures in the net, we can assume some of them will be tiny, some already dead, some unclean under Jewish dietary laws, and some just too gross to sell or eat. The image suggests we're to imagine *everyone* and *everything* getting gathered together and sorted. The Kingdom's culmination somehow resembles this picture of a universal, comprehensive reckoning.

Jesus doesn't explain what makes something in the net "bad," but the word in question has a sense of "rotten" or "decayed," as if it's already dead or dying. Clearly we're talking about fish—or other things—that are utterly undesirable. The undesirable things aren't "bad" because they're occasionally selfish or rude to the other fish. Something's *really bad* about them. The sorting reveals the true nature of things, so one kind can be removed from another.

At the end of the parable Jesus interprets the comparison for us. The full arrival of the Kingdom, "at the end of the age," will involve revealing the full truth. It will be when God, with the help of God's angels ("angel" means ambassador or agent), reveals what's "evil" and *pulls it away* from what's "righteous." Jesus likens the rotten seafood and pollution in the net to evil people or evil forces. It raises the question of what he means by what's "evil." Clearly there's more malice going on there than someone who skips church too many times, blasts their gas-powered leaf blower early on Saturday mornings, or roots for the Los Angeles Dodgers. God lets angels make the judgments of what constitutes "evil." God doesn't commission us to do the sorting.

Jesus never mentions what happens to the "good" fish that get sorted into baskets on the beach. If I were one of them, I'd like to be thrown back into the sea, especially now that the problematic creatures have been taken out of my habitat. The parable emphasizes the sorting as a time of truth-telling. That's about it. It's a sorting. Don't add details. Jesus isn't planning to have delicious, righteous fish breaded and sautéed with garlic in God's kingdom. We shouldn't push any parable's symbolism too far, or it gets strange. Every metaphor breaks down when overstretched, just like you can ruin a poem if you take it too literally.

There's more. The fate of "the evil," as the parable describes it, is grim. Fire. Weeping. Gnashing of teeth. Try not to import the imagery you've accumulated from Dante and *The Far Side*. I mean, don't overdraw what Jesus says at the parable's conclusion. It's disturbing, but it's not without similar passages in Matthew (see, for example, 7:19; 13:40-42; 22:13; 24:30). The bottom line, from this parable's perspective, is that undesirable or corrosive things have been tossed out, at least for now, in a most decisive way, never to return.

Matthew's larger message says more than any one parable can communicate. Imagine if this parable was the only teaching that Jesus's earliest followers passed down to us. We'd have a very different Christianity today, probably one full of fear and anxiety. We'd all be terrified of God, and we'd have no good sense of what Jesus wants from us or wants to give us.

Matthew's larger message says more than any one parable can communicate.

No single parable can tell the whole story about Jesus and the Kingdom. If one could, then Jesus would have told it over and over. Various parables illustrate various aspects of his message. It's usually up to us, the readers, to discuss what we think the parable means to illustrate, as well as what it seems not to be talking about.

What should we learn from the dragnet, then? Jesus is saying that the full arrival of the Kingdom will—and must—entail the elimination of dangerous things. God is committed to root out things that are rotten and things that do damage. He's especially concerned, as other parts of Matthew confirm, when threatening things or counterfeit things are mixed together with things that are "good" or "righteous."

In the parable of the sheep and the goats (25:31-46), which we explored in chapter 1, the people Jesus calls "righteous" are merciful people. In that context Jesus doesn't mean they're "perfect" or specially "chosen." Nor are they "sanctimonious" or "judgmental." The "righteous" are those who prioritize compassion. He's concerned about the things that prevent righteous compassion from thriving. As we'll see in chapter 5, he believes that some of those things come from misguided leadership and counterfeit forms of righteousness. From the parable of the dragnet, we can observe, at minimum, that Jesus expresses a commitment to see the world cleansed of corrupt things.

You may have noticed I keep saying "things." Isn't Jesus talking about people? He might be. If he is, then he's still talking about more than people. I'm trying to steer us away from simply presuming that the main problem Jesus sees in the world is its people, taken as individuals. We may be inclined to imagine Mother Theresa being placed in the "good" fish basket with a harp, while Stalin gets tossed into the furnace with his accordion. Erase that thought and leave individuals aside for a moment. What if the unclean, diseased, or undesirable things in the parable's net represent the oppressive cosmic forces that the New Testament calls demons? Or what about social ills that cause horrible suffering, such as systemic racism, HIV, and corporate greed? I have to think Jesus is in favor of a world without antisemitism, fetal alcohol syndrome, misogyny, and antisocial personality disorders. That doesn't mean he has written off individuals who suffer from—or contribute to—those things. It means those destructive forces or phenomena won't exist within God's kingdom.

I'm not glossing over what Jesus says about destruction being a part of the reckoning to come. I want to illustrate that how you interpret the judgment envisioned in this parable will depend also on how you answer several complicated questions: what sin is, what causes human brokenness, how people break free from our attraction to false gods, and who's to blame in a world that conditions us to prey on one another so it feels like it's everyone's fault and no one's particular fault at the same time. You and I might come to different conclusions about those topics. But Matthew won't let us avoid them altogether. Jesus promises: God will judge. That doesn't mean God has it out for certain people. Rather, God is determined to make sure righteousness has its full effects.

Reflections

It's only chapter 2 and you might be asking, "Why are we talking about judgment so much in a book that's supposed to be about Jesus's 'promised blessings'?" Let me assure you, even with all of the passages that promise judgment, Matthew still tells a story brimming with promised blessings.

The challenge before us is understanding that God's commitment to judgment is a dimension of God's abundant love. Let's rephrase that, to make it less abstract: God's commitment to revealing the truth about the world and its people is part and parcel of God's unshakable love for the world and its people.

There are a number of promises at the heart of the good news Jesus shares with the world. Two basic ones are: (1) God loves the world, especially people who experience the indignities of poverty, suffering, exclusion, and abuse; (2) God is determined to rectify the state of affairs that causes so much misery. Those aren't brand-new ideas that Jesus reveals; they were already deeply ingrained in Judaism before Jesus's birth. God's fierce commitment to humanity's well-being expresses itself in many ways throughout the Bible. In Exodus, for example, God fights—with deadly consequences for Pharaoh's army—on behalf of the Hebrews to free them from slavery. In a similar vein, Jesus promises the transformation of the world order, exposing and eliminating whatever hinders human flourishing.

If God doesn't fix what's wrong in the grand scheme of things, the promises we reviewed in chapter 1 ring hollow. Without God's judgment, Jesus's mercy does little more than offer good wishes.

Promises of judgment are promises to end the torments that afflict persecuted and oppressed people. Remember that Jesus promises, in Matthew 5, "Blessed are the meek, for they will inherit the earth." For that to happen, he first has to make the earth safe from whatever jackals are roaming the world, hungry to snack on the meek. Something has to change.

If the world is a harsh place, as a quick scan of today's news probably confirms, then divine love without judgment just gives people company in their unending misery.

If the world is a harsh place, and it is, then divine judgment without love will end up consuming all of us. No one's an absolutely righteous fish all on their own.

Jesus's promises of judgment don't cancel God's graciousness. They can't. They mean we leave the judgment up to God, trusting that divine love extends to us and even to our enemies, if indeed we even have enemies.

Jesus's promises of judgment don't cancel God's graciousness.

As I said earlier, it's difficult to talk about divine judgment. I struggle with it. Can't God simply nudge the whole world toward being a better place through the power of divine love? Sometimes that happens. I've observed transformations in individuals, families, and communities. That alone reminds me never to underestimate God's ability and desire to repair, with grace, whatever has become broken. In the New Testament's imagination, however, there's still something stubbornly persistent about evil. Martin Luther's famous hymn, "A Mighty Fortress," views the world through a New Testament lens with this lyric: "And though this world, with devils filled, should threaten to undo us..." I personally don't believe that the world is teeming with unseen demons, but I do know that evil—wherever it comes from and however it manifests itself—is unflinching, never giving up without a fight. The New Testament, generally speaking, understands wickedness as more organic and more sinister than just the bad choices individuals make.

Finally, you've probably sensed my discomfort with terms such as *hell* and *the furnace of fire*, which appear in passages about future judgment. Obviously this Gospel means to seize our attention. Nevertheless, situated where we stand in history, I contend that traditional imagery and metaphors for talking about punishment, like those terms, have become unhelpful.

For one thing, Matthew's depiction of Jesus's teachings doesn't come with explicit renderings of judgment, consequences, and annihilation. When we turn images and symbols into literal descriptions, as the church has done with many of these, we break them. Furthermore, I don't think Matthew tells us that we all have to agree about whether Satan, hell, and demons exist or how else we might explain how individuals, societies, systems, rulers, and social policies become destructive. The Gospel simply doesn't spend time spelling out those topics. But Matthew is clear where it comes to reassuring us that God, through Jesus Christ, will create a different, harmonious, and safe future. If that's true, then bring on the truth-telling of a trustworthy and benevolent God. Let truth be told, and let the people who suffer the most find freedom from their oppression.

In the meantime, I and others who live more comfortable lives can prepare by telling the truth about ourselves and our own habits of resisting God's righteous kingdom. Truth often hurts, yet it's part of healing. We tell the hard truths about ourselves best in the presence of God and one another. We do so trusting God to mend both our hearts and the little circles of the world where we reside, one day at a time.

Chapter 3

A Vision for the Church and World

Passages to Explore:

Jesus, it appears, was a dreamer. He seems uninterested in incremental change toward a better world. He dreams of remaking it, not so human society as we know it disappears, but so our shared existence becomes entirely safe and bountiful for all, harmonious, displaying the goodwill and holiness of God.

Accordingly, Jesus provides no step-by-step guides toward better living or becoming more generous. His ministry shocks us into a new orientation, yanking our consciousness from one reality into a kind of alternate reality—one so different we didn't know it was possible. How we get to that new reality will be up to him. But first he wants us to perceive it, crave it, and pray for it. He also prepares us to anticipate it in our lives, through our trust in him and our conduct toward one another.

Jesus provides no step-by-step guides toward better living or becoming more generous.

As Jesus communicates his vision for a different future, the notion of the "church" emerges as an important vehicle—really, a community—for his dream to take flight. It's a conspicuous feature of Matthew, for the word *church* doesn't appear in the other three Gospels. Jesus explicitly gives a name to the distinctive community his followers join (the Greek word translated "church" simply means any assembly or congress of people who come together for a purpose).

Jesus never says that the assembly of his followers will be faultless or that the church is the only setting where his values manifest themselves. The church mustn't seek dominance in the world, and it shouldn't understand itself as a morally superior sect. The church should be a community known for its concern for vulnerable people and for its commitment to reconciliation. Those qualities of the church, if it operates as it ought to, won't change the world on their own, but they certainly point in the right direction.

As we explore several passages, remember to put aside the question *What do these verses want me to do?* First consider, instead, *What kind of world does Jesus promise? What vision resides in his mind?* The alternate reality he describes may seem too good to be possible, but that never slows down a dreamer.

Matthew 5:17–6:1

("But I Say to You...")

We're not yet finished with the Sermon on the Mount. Rather, it isn't finished with us. Let's visit one more section of Jesus's rich inaugural address. In this passage Jesus lays out very high expectations for human behavior. He's not trying to be strict and demanding as much as he's envisioning a world in which God's desire for human flourishing comes to full expression. Imagine his mood as excited and hopeful, not austere and strict. Picture him saying, "Don't you want to be part of a world where everyone treats everyone else with the greatest honor?"

Jesus situates himself and his vision for the world squarely within his Judaism. He doesn't toss out "the Law or the Prophets," which, as I noted in chapter 2, were (and still are) segments of Jewish scriptures. His aim to "fulfill" those writings doesn't mean to end them but to elevate their hopes to an even fuller expression. I cannot overstate the importance of Christians remembering that Jesus participated and taught within the Jewish mainstream of his time. In all the Gospels he debates issues that interested other Jewish teachers, and he shows great respect for God's law (Torah). As with other Jews, he views Torah not as a list of burdensome prohibitions meant to stifle or shame people but as an invitation to a way of living that aligns with God's best intentions for humanity.

Jesus imagines God's kingdom as a state of affairs marked by righteousness, which he characterizes as more than moral correctness but specifically as commitment to one another's well-being. A person's righteousness should be on par with that of the scribes and Pharisees, which is saying a lot. We'll discuss Jesus's criticisms of those groups in chapter 5, but for now be aware that hardly anyone in Jesus's orbit would deny the scribes' and Pharisees' devotion to God's righteousness.

Later, at the end of this passage, Jesus tells his audience to "be perfect" (5:48). Uh oh. That appears to rule out a lot of us, but keep reading. We often assume that "perfect" equals "no moral flaws whatsoever," yet the English words *complete* and *whole* come closer to capturing the Greek word in question. The idea is about living lives that fully reflect God's desires. That's what this entire section of Jesus's sermon means to describe.

I won't go into detail about what's said in 5:21-47. There's a lot happening there. Let's focus on the larger picture. In general Jesus affirms certain laws we find in Torah every time he says, "You have heard that it was said…" (The exception is in 5:43, for no Old Testament passage says, "Hate your enemy.") All the commands he cites have to do with our conduct toward one another, either fostering or destroying trustworthy relationships. He's interested in a world where people treat each other justly, which entails not taking advantage of anyone. After affirming each law, he enlarges its scope when he says, "But I say to you…" He demands more. He envisions more. He's not criticizing Torah; he's lamenting a broken world. The unifying thread is simple to understand although difficult to achieve: go out of your way to take care of each other.

What kind of world does Jesus want? Avoiding murder isn't enough; we should also stop short of anger. He forbids lust as well as adultery. He commands us to seek the good of our enemies through prayer. These aren't minor matters. Jesus knows the corrosive power of hatred, desperation, objectification, deception, and greed. Those powers ruin families, businesses, friendships, and nations.

In these verses we also encounter some of the judgment imagery we've discussed. Clearly Jesus isn't joking, but he also knows how high his vision sets the bar. Nevertheless, don't take this small part of the sermon as his sole and final word on anything and everything. He also has plenty to say about forgiveness in Matthew.

Some readers assume that Jesus lays a trap here. They claim he's making Torah even more impossible to observe, because he wants us to fail and therefore discover how sinful we are. If he sets an impossible standard, we'll recognize our (and Torah's) shortcomings and run to him for forgiveness. The argument goes, "The law's too hard, so don't even try. Recognize you're a sinner who can't satisfy God's stringent demands." That interpretation is mistaken. It misunderstands how Torah and its laws function within Judaism. Moreover, it perversely implies that Jesus *really* wants us to discover what useless worms he thinks we are before he's willing to help us out. It's a perspective that misreads both Jesus's heart and the sermon's focus.

Contrary to that point of view, the sermon isn't a judge's guilty verdict. It's a dreamer's manifesto. Jesus unfolds his vision of a beautiful world marked by trust, justice, and security. He invites us to imagine it with him.

My friend Mary Hinkle Shore, who's also a New Testament scholar, is the first person I heard describe the Sermon on the Mount as Jesus's "I Have a Dream" speech. Her allusion to the Rev. Dr. Martin Luther King Jr. is intentional. King's famous 1963 speech insists that the promises of the Declaration of Independence, the US Constitution, and Abraham Lincoln's Emancipation Proclamation remain magnificent promises even though they haven't been fully actualized. He and his fellow Black citizens received bad checks from America, but he believes the "bank" of those historic documents still holds promises that can pay out liberty. He therefore dreams confidently of a future in which America will deliver all its promised richness, even if that future sounds far-fetched in 1963.

Jesus is up to something similar, insofar as he sees Torah holding divine promises about love, respect, and goodwill that he wants to see completely realized. He wants Torah's vision perfected or made whole. He's eager for a society whose people go out of their way to protect lives and relationships. He, therefore, denounces behaviors and attitudes that harm or take advantage of others. He says, in effect, "Imagine this fantastic way with me. Everyone will thrive in a system like that. It's God's desire."

Don't worry, I'm still a Presbyterian who believes we need lots of help and forgiveness. By ourselves we'll never work our way into the world Jesus imagines. (I should say, too, that Jews also believe in a gracious God who forgives their inevitable failings.) Jesus also knows, you'll recall, a thing or two about human frailty and our "little faith." Shortly we'll explore what he says about reconciliation and the difficulties of bearing with one another. Before working on solutions, though, he paints a picture of the righteousness, peacefulness, and radical kindheartedness he has in mind. Before he takes you where you need to go, he wants you on his side.

Finally, in 6:1, Jesus discourages people from seeking their way into God's intentions all on their own power and with a public brashness that gives "righteousness" a bad name. Jesus despises sanctimony in Matthew. He says "practicing" righteousness must occur in private, not public. If you're doing it for show, don't bother. Otherwise it's a performance and not an exercise that will change your heart. Later, in 6:2-18, he will specifically commend almsgiving, prayer, and fasting in private.

Remember, he says to *practice*. He wants us to have a little experience in humility under our belts as we witness his dream finally come to fulfillment.

Matthew 9:35–10:25

(Compassionate Connections in an Often Inhospitable World)

The Sermon on the Mount doesn't stand alone in Matthew. On at least four other occasions Jesus gives an extended speech. Taken together, they emphasize his role as a teacher. In Matthew's tenth chapter, Jesus offers lengthy instruction to twelve of his disciples (his "apostles," or ambassadors) before they go out and wield his authority over the damaging power of "unclean spirits" and "every disease and every sickness" (10:1).

Jesus commissions his followers to extend the reach of his ministry immediately after "he saw the crowds." (The exact same phrase appears in 5:1, too, where the sight of the crowds prompts him to lay out his vision in the Sermon on the Mount.) The crowds appear worn down, "harassed and helpless." Comparing them to "sheep without a shepherd," Jesus implies their leaders have failed them, for the Bible regularly uses shepherds as a metaphor for kings and other political or priestly authorities (for example, Numbers 27:15-20; 2 Samuel 5:1-3; Jeremiah 23:1-4). Those who might devote their power to easing the masses' miseries either cannot or will not. The work that Jesus calls his people to perform begins as a rebuke of the cruelty and apathy that often infects our societies.

The work that Jesus calls his people to perform begins as a rebuke of the cruelty and apathy that often infects our societies.

Jesus does not, at least in this speech, send the Twelve out to enlarge the church's membership. His command to make additional disciples comes later in Matthew, after his resurrection. The church's primary mission is mercy and connection. It still is. Such a focus makes sense. For any church to be *Jesus's* church, as Matthew understands it, it has to be committed to spreading mercy and fostering positive relationships. Jesus's good news reiterates the God of Israel's long-standing commitment to nourishing life and loving one's neighbor.

Jesus tells his Jewish followers to begin by connecting with other Jews. The command for them to stick to Jewish audiences presents some practical challenges, since most Jews around the Sea of Galilee lived in proximity to Gentiles. As we'll see in chapter 4, the mission will widen soon enough.

One aspect of what Jesus says about his followers' work has fascinating implications. They carry his own ministry forward. In Jesus's vision for the church, his followers share—they don't merely imitate—

the restorative and compassionate work of Jesus. Jesus indicates this by instructing his followers to perform actions he has done already, as narrated in Matthew 8–9. He empowers them to demonstrate the Kingdom's power to set things right. They are to free people from the spiritual, physical, and social forces that steal human wholeness and dignity. Jesus himself inserts his followers into opportunities where divine grace can manifest itself. As other passages in Matthew also affirm, Jesus promises to be present among us as we do this work.

The church plays a role in promising the blessings Jesus provides. His vision for the world involves a church that offers an antidote to the indifference that the world and its leaders too often inflict on those who suffer. Jesus never says that the church is the only source of blessings for the world, so no one should get too full of themselves or too suspicious of others who also spread mercy.

Furthermore, Jesus acknowledges that the work will be neither easy nor glamorous. His followers' capacity to be conduits of his compassion will be tested. He, therefore, sends them out as guests, not as people looking to claim a platform or impose their will on others. Their marching orders prioritize humility; their basic appearance and empty pockets declare their utter dependence on Jesus and the kindness of strangers. They mustn't jump from house to house, seeking more comfortable beds and more spacious lodging if other potential hosts offer.

Anticipate rejection, discouragement, and danger, warns Jesus. Some people don't like it when powerless, sickly, and ignored people regain their health, dignity, and voice. The status quo works when certain folks remain disenfranchised, and the status quo doesn't appreciate disruption. Jesus therefore urges his people to trust that God accompanies them.

My favorite detail about this speech is how it eventually ends, in 11:1: "Now when Jesus had finished instructing his twelve disciples, he went on from there to teach and proclaim his message in their cities." In other words, Matthew gives us a long speech about what

Jesus's disciples should do and then never narrates them doing what they're told to. The story immediately reverts back to *Jesus's* activity. It's humorous. Readers rightly wonder, "How did they, the Twelve, do? Did it work?" We don't know. Matthew keeps the focus on Jesus. His story is too busy to slow down.

I like Matthew's omission of the disciples' adventures because it denies us a chance to observe them taking a victory lap or celebrating successes (as in Luke 10:17-20). I don't dislike the Twelve. I just appreciate that Matthew denies us a sense of triumphalism in this moment. We in the church should take confidence in the knowledge that Christ is busy and attentive with us, before us, and behind us— and sometimes apart from us. But that knowledge cannot devolve into arrogance. If we slip into thinking that Jesus's ministry somehow belongs to us, the church easily forgets its purpose. History teaches us how dangerous a conceited church can be.

Given my concerns, I also appreciate that Jesus's speech envisions his followers as guests in other people's homes. Guests don't presume they already know what's best for hosts. The detail encourages me to rethink the discussions about hospitality that occur in congregations today. We need to recognize that when Jesus talks about hospitality, he means dropping one's defenses and opening oneself up to the richness of other people. It's not about what "we" do for "them." Too often I hear folks speak of hospitality as a kind of strategy for the church's growth, yet for them the hospitality still flows in only one direction: we give and others receive; we invite and they assimilate. There's nothing wrong with charity and welcome; most congregations could improve at both. Too often, however, the dynamics we describe as "hospitality" take shape as paternalism, in which "we" have resources that "they" should tap into for their benefit. What if we took time to honor the gifts and dreams of others? What if we listen more than we speak?

Jesus might be the rare savior who avoids the trap of taking on a savior complex.

Matthew 18:1-14

(Protecting Vulnerable Sheep)

Jesus also has expectations for what kind of community the church should cultivate within itself. He envisions a lived, embodied expression of mutual care and reconciliation. All of Matthew 18 communicates that vision through an extended speech Jesus gives, which is another of this Gospel's five long speeches. Jesus instructs the church not to let anyone slip through the cracks.

He begins by focusing on children. His followers should imitate childlike humility. Jesus isn't praising people who act modestly or who have reserved and polite demeanors. In the ancient world, most children lacked any real social standing. Many of them died very young. They had few if any legal rights and privileges. When Jesus tells his followers to be "humble like this child," he has vulnerability in mind. He tells us to surrender power and reject any kind of me-first attitude.

If I were present in this scene I'd get impatient and foolishly try to help Jesus out: "Wait a minute, Jesus. If I make it my top priority to put everyone else's well-being ahead of my own, what's to prevent me from being taken advantage of by someone else? What you're saying puts people at risk, right?" He'd tell me, kindly I hope, to back off and let him finish.

Jesus goes on to warn anyone who would misuse his humility principle to hurt or exploit others. If you make a child or someone with childlike humility stumble—if you put something harmful in front of someone like that—Jesus says he'd prefer that you go jump in a lake. With a massive millstone necklace. The imagery suggests you've committed a terrible offense.

The humble disposition Jesus desires only works, therefore, if *everyone* participates. In that case, others in the community will always be looking out for one another. The community of Jesus's followers must be a sanctuary. If that sounds impossible, remember Jesus is a dreamer. In any case, his seriousness about stumbling blocks should urge us to run from any leader in the church who commands people to ignore their rights, dignity, or safety and to subject themselves to exploitative and abusive people. Such a leader has failed to comprehend the kind of community Jesus has in mind.

To illustrate the depths of his concern, Jesus offers a parable about God's unshakable resolve when it comes to protecting those who find themselves at risk. This parable about a lost sheep also appears in Luke 15:1-7, but there the story makes an entirely different point; it's about God's determination to bring a wayward person to repentance and the celebration that should follow. Here, in Matthew, Jesus specifies that the parable highlights God's intention to prevent "one of these little ones" (a child, a model of powerlessness) from falling away from the protection found in the flock (the church).

If you're wondering why the same parable might have two different functions in two different Gospels, let me assure you that preachers know how to reuse a good story when they've got one.

Jesus never explains how or why one sheep goes "astray." Maybe its wandering symbolizes doing something wrong, or straying from the path, as we might say. The context suggests to me instead that the sheep just somehow got separated. The rest of the flock wasn't looking out for it. (We're dealing with *sheep*, remember. We shouldn't expect much intelligence or awareness from them.) In any case, a lone sheep has little chance of surviving, and so the shepherd springs into action. He refuses to cut his losses and accept the casualty of even 1 percent of the flock. He brings the sheep back, rejoicing, returning it from danger to security. God shows intense dedication to someone who becomes vulnerable; the community of Jesus's followers should do likewise.

Of course, churches should not be so concerned about their own internal culture that they devolve into insular, closed-off communities. At the same time, I know some churches that talk about outreach and evangelism so much that they seem to have forgotten how important it is to make their own congregation a safe place where love and reconciliation happen. Remember, the church's primary mission is mercy and connection. There's little reason to hope anyone will stick around if a congregation isn't prioritizing those things for the sake of everyone who comes through its doors.

Matthew 18:15-20

(Keeping the Church Safe)

A streak of realism weaves itself through Jesus's dreamy visions for the church and world. He doesn't ignore the difficulties that come with trying to coexist and cooperate with others. Conflict inevitably arises, and people hurt one another even when they're all trying to follow Jesus. With practical instructions about those matters, Jesus restates his ongoing commitment to providing a place where everyone can thrive. Jesus's church cannot be a community that deals from a deck stacked against people who have less clout or fewer advantages.

The scenario he imagines involves a person who sins against someone else. The issue demands careful attention because it extends beyond misunderstandings, disagreements, or simmering tensions. The teachings in this passage aren't a command for the church to confront anyone who fails to live up to a certain ethical standard. Rather, something personal has happened. Likewise, Jesus's concern escalates if reconciliation doesn't occur quickly. When a perpetrator—the one who "sins against" another—refuses to admit or repair the damage they have done, Jesus calls for an intensified response that brings more members of the church into the equation. The circumstances sound severe: imagine persons who simply refuse to own up to the harm they have caused, even when a cluster of additional people attest to the damage.

Unfortunately, what I'm describing is alarmingly easy to imagine. Jesus's hypothetical situation occurs too frequently.

Jesus says that a bullheaded and unrepentant offender should be treated like "a gentile and a tax collector"—an outsider who deserves to be shunned. Before you start fantasizing about whom you might want to boot out of your church, however, notice two things. First, Jesus himself likes reaching out to tax collectors and gentiles (see 9:10; 11:19; 12:18). Second, the next part of Jesus's extended speech proclaims the importance of forgiveness. At the same time, the wrongdoer in Jesus's scenario comes across as more than a casual or misunderstood offender. This person denies responsibility and refuses to attempt reconciliation. Predator, harasser, or gaslighter strike me as more fitting descriptors. An extreme case? Perhaps. But Jesus knows that religious communities often harbor people who enjoy bullying others.

I've heard Christians appeal to this passage as a template for how you might lovingly confront someone who's out of control or might create a process for resolving conflicts in an organization or community. Jesus's teachings could prove helpful for those purposes, but the passage's main objective is to underscore the need for a church to provide an environment in which people are not mistreated or taken advantage of by others. It must remain a community committed to fostering reconciliation among its people. Jesus insists that Christians who have been sinned-against by other Christians must have recourse, lest some individuals, groups, or leaders make a habit of hurting others.

We have no choice but to remain committed to being a community devoted to reconciliation and restoration.

Jesus imagines the church not as an institution trying to gut it out on the strength of its own moral energy or entrepreneurial creativity but as a community in which he resides. "Where two or three are gathered" (18:20) in Jesus's name, he dwells among them. He summons the church to guard its identity as a place where people who are "poor in spirit" or "pure in heart" (5:3, 8) can be empowered by love, acceptance, and solidarity in the presence of Christ himself. The church inevitably stumbles in its commitment to provide the sanctuary that Jesus promises. But because he remains literally present among his people, we have no choice but to remain committed to being a community devoted to reconciliation and restoration.

Matthew 18:21-35
(The Power and Pains of Forgiveness)

Forgiveness can change the world. It renews relationships, repairs generational trauma, and improves one's psychological health. It's also extremely difficult. Especially when it's rushed, it can put injured people at risk for new injuries. We need to treat the challenges associated with forgiveness carefully, even as we recognize that in Matthew Jesus lifts up forgiveness as a key marker of the church's common life. In his vision, the church is a community where no one holds a sincere person's past against them. As you might expect, Jesus speaks about God forgiving sins several times in Matthew (6:12, 14; 9:2; 12:31), and once he refers to forgiveness in connection to his crucifixion (26:28; see also 1:21). He also knows the power of people forgiving other people.

A short exchange with Peter (18:21-22) introduces the topic. Jesus blows Peter's expectation out of the water, telling him to keep on forgiving anyone who sins against him. The expression Jesus uses is unclear: he speaks of forgiving either seventy-seven times or four hundred ninety times ("seventy times seven"). He's using hyperbole; he doesn't expect you to keep count.

Speaking of hyperbole, the parable he tells next contains a mountain of it. The first enslaved man in Jesus's short story owes the king a gazillion dollars. Really it says ten thousand talents, but one talent equals about fifteen years of a laborer's wages. The man in the parable would need over fifty million days of toil to pay his debt. Everyone would laugh when hearing Jesus name the figure, because the amount is ludicrous. That's the point.

Astonishingly, the king forgives the entire debt. The enslaved man, however, remains unchanged by the avalanche of mercy, for he punishes another enslaved man who cannot repay him one hundred denarii, roughly a laborer's wages over one hundred days. The parable has a gruesome ending, with the king resorting to torturing the first man until he can repay an unpayable sum—an impossible expectation. There's also a warning that Jesus's followers had better forgive each other too.

Right away we sense that the parable doesn't fully add up. It's strange. The first enslaved man has no conscience. As for the king, he reverses his forgiveness, which implies he never really forgave in the first place. At the end of the parable, everyone looks bad. That's probably part of Jesus's objective. The parable's ambiguities confirm how complicated forgiveness is. The relationships between showing mercy to our debtors and trespassers on one hand and enduring the consequences of our own debts and trespasses on the other hand are never simple. Don't take my discussion of this peculiar parable to imply that forgiveness is uncomplicated. Whatever this parable illustrates, it hardly captures the full character of what forgiveness entails or why anyone should do it.

If I haven't yet convinced you that the parable has limitations, think about the problems of comparing forgiveness to canceled debt. Financial restitution works when someone breaks my window or steals my car when I'm not using it. But what price can you place on broken trust or the loss of a person's psychological health? Some wounds can't be quantified. Some never heal. To compare forgiveness to canceling an IOU or updating a spreadsheet doesn't tell the whole story.

Instead, the parable has more to say about a person's *experience* of forgiveness. Whether it's being forgiven or extending forgiveness to others—forgiveness has the potential to change a person. Being forgiven by God sets us in new directions. Better directions. Being forgiven by someone else should affect how we treat others. My attempts to forgive a person should change me too.

However—and the parable speaks directly to this reality—sometimes we simply aren't capable of grasping that forgiveness can transform our outlook on our neighbors and on the offenses that make living in this world so difficult.

Most of my students are on the road to becoming pastors. I remind them that people rarely find forgiving others (or themselves) as easy as our theology can make it sound. I have a few basic convictions I impress upon them, since they'll be preaching and teaching about forgiveness. First, forgiving someone rarely happens through a one-time action. Forgiveness happens progressively and sometimes slowly and indirectly. It's not unusual for a forgiver to have to restart from the beginning.

Second, forgiveness doesn't mean forgetting the past or acting as if no harm ever occurred. To forgive involves accepting that the past is the past and trying to keep it in the past. Moving on from the past doesn't mean erasing it. Pains and distrust may linger forever, often for sound reasons, and so the relationship shared by a sinner and a sinned-against may have to change. At least hope remains for a forgiver to open themselves up to a new future, even if the perpetrator is out of the picture.

Third, if you press a person to forgive someone else and be reconciled with them, you may put that person in danger or reawaken trauma. Whatever it means for a person to move into a new future, forgiveness shouldn't entail their revictimization.

Jesus's parable reads like a tragedy, because none of its characters moves past the severe calculus of debt and punishment. Grudges and resentment crowd out the possibility of new beginnings. No one experiences change or the transformative power of grace.

What does this mean for Jesus's vision of the church and the world? The parable gives no assurance that the church can be a community of quick or painless forgiveness. Jesus's words to Peter nevertheless summon us to cultivate a culture that embraces the process of practicing interpersonal forgiveness and maintaining space for people to struggle with it. The church must rejoice in the new futures that forgiveness creates and also respect the healing processes that need to occur for people to forgive, whether they're considering what it takes to forgive others or themselves.

Practice is a good verb for us to use with respect to forgiveness. It acknowledges that we experience progress and setbacks while we work toward a new future. For that kind of practice to occur—where people work truthfully through tough questions of pain, guilt, accountability, and conflict—the church needs to be committed to nurturing everyone within its wide circle. If a hopeful new future is possible for our fractured selves, just like the future Jesus envisions in his sermons, Jesus will be the one to lead us there.

Reflections

The next chapter will continue our exploration of what's involved in following Jesus. It will sketch a fuller picture of what it means to attach oneself to his plans for a restored world and a humanity that bathes in the benefits of God's righteousness.

At the same time, I won't lead us away from the idealism that pulses through Jesus's vision of what's possible. We sometimes react cautiously to Jesus's grand promises since we don't want to downplay the struggles of humanity's complicated existence. We can't dwell in utopian fantasies. If we're honest, we grow skeptical that Jesus really means it when he promises to bring his blessings to those who need them the most. The church tends to withdraw, settle for too little, and avoid risk.

The passages we considered in this chapter shake us from complacency.

The passages we considered in this chapter shake us from complacency. They insist that Christian faith carries an inherent dissatisfaction with the shortcomings and inequities of our world.

They urge us to care more, to expect more from God, and to imbue our congregations with a purpose that focuses on welcoming Jesus in every stranger who needs refuge.

If only embodying Jesus's vision was as effortless as writing and talking about it. I make no claims that any of these lessons about supporting other people's well-being comes easily to me. I've not met many people who are really good at it, but usually the ones who are manage to practice their acts of mercy, connection, inclusion, and forgiveness under the radar. You sometimes have to search for them.

Jesus doesn't demand spotless moral perfection from the church, nor from each of his followers. I'd wager he's nevertheless wounded by any church whose sense of mission doesn't involve eagerly accepting people as they are and making space for them to belong within a flawed but caring congregational community. In a time when so many churches chase after consultants, surveys, and trendy strategies, Jesus asks us to commit ourselves to making our congregations into sanctuaries and sites of forgiveness and reconciliation. He promises we aren't working at it alone.

Chapter 4

Participating as Disciples

Passages to Explore:

Matthew 1:1-17	(Jesus's Genealogy)
Matthew 9:9-13	(Mercy toward Matthew and His Ilk)
Matthew 11:28-30	(Easy Yoke, Light Burden)
Matthew 12:15-21	(Jesus's Appeal to the Crowds)
Matthew 15:29-31	(Crowds, Again)
Matthew 28:16-20	(The Great Commission)

Matthew's consistent focus on Jesus means that many other people in the story remain anonymous or confined to the edges. You may be familiar with the names Peter, James, and John, who enjoy the most prominence among the twelve men we often refer to as *the* disciples. But Matthew wants us to notice many other disciples, too.

The word *disciple* doesn't signal anything special or uniquely spiritual by itself. The Greek word in question means simply "pupil," "student," or "adherent." In that regard, all ancient teachers—except perhaps the really bad ones whom no one liked—had disciples.

It's fair to refer to Mary Magdalene and another Mary (the mother of two guys named James and Joseph) as Jesus's disciples, too, for they follow and support Jesus throughout his ministry (27:55-56). He asks many other people to "follow" in his way (see 8:22; 16:24; 19:21), and many do (see 4:25; 8:1; 12:15; 19:2; 20:34). As we saw in the previous chapter, associating oneself with Jesus isn't about basking in his glory and kindness. It involves getting pulled into the vision he has for a new world.

This chapter goes hand in hand with chapter 3. It focuses on episodes when Jesus calls people to himself or characterizes what life with him is about. What should shine more brightly throughout our explorations of several passages—most of which are brief—is our sense of how welcoming and magnetic Jesus is. As we observe the ways Matthew depicts life with Jesus, some of the promised blessings I highlighted in chapter 1 will appear less abstract to us. Matthew depicts those blessings enfleshed, or lived out, through Jesus's actions.

> **The kingdom of God is anything but an exclusive club for insiders or people who have it all together.**

Performing excruciating work and heroic deeds don't define life with Jesus, according to Matthew's depiction. Accompanying Jesus (or, rather, being accompanied by him) does. Maybe most important, this affiliation with him—this discipleship—includes a wide array of people. Jesus becomes known by the company he keeps, and that company repeatedly signals to us that the kingdom of God is anything but an exclusive club for insiders or people who have it all together.

Matthew 1:1-17
(Jesus's Genealogy)

In Matthew, Jesus doesn't summon anyone to become a disciple or follower until 4:18-22, but from the opening verses this Gospel prepares us to comprehend that anyone can find their way into playing a part in what he's up to. If you're expecting strict qualifications for what it takes to associate with him, expect instead to be surprised.

The opening verses offer a list of names, a genealogy covering forty-two generations. If you suffer from anxiety dreams about having to give a speech in front of a crowd, wait until you read this passage and consider the prospect of being asked to pronounce all the names of Jesus's ancestors during the Scripture reading before the sermon next Sunday. (For the record, Zerubbabel is my favorite one to say aloud.)

It's an impressive list, with some names that Bible readers will recognize. It connects Jesus to Abraham and God's initial promise to create and guide a nation, King David of Israel's glory years, and the pain and restoration of the Babylonian Exile. Jesus is as Jewish as you can imagine. In Luke 3:23-38 we find a similar but not identical genealogy. Like other legal genealogies included in the Bible, Jesus's genealogies record the names of male relatives. It wasn't until later in history, after Jesus, that some Jewish groups started tracking a person's Jewishness though their mother, in a system called matrilineal descent. The polish and formality of the genealogies in Matthew and Luke underscore Jesus's authority and raise expectations about what God will do next through the son of Mary.

Except, maybe we should back up and reread Matthew's genealogy a little more slowly. It's actually not as uniform and tidy as I made it out to be. There are four women scattered in it among the men, plus Jesus's mother Mary at the end. Their names are Tamar, Rahab, Ruth, and Bathsheba (who is referred to not by name but as "the wife of Uriah"). Of course, there's nothing shameful about including women in one's genealogy, especially these famous women. Nevertheless, as we will see, their sheer presence suggests Matthew isn't interested in steering around controversy or limiting its good news to credentialed insiders. The Gospel's opening message is: "You might be surprised by who belongs in Jesus's story."

Some people like to point out that sexual scandals—or, at the least, "irregular sexual unions" as a footnote in my thick study Bible puts it—were prominent aspects of the four women's biblical histories. Their stories are more complicated than I can explain here, but to summarize briefly: Tamar, mistaken for a prostitute, sleeps with her father-in-law in an attempt to expose the injustice he perpetrated against her (Genesis 38); Rahab, a prostitute in Jericho, allows a pair of Hebrew spies (who may also be customers) to hide in her home (Joshua 2); Ruth is a widow and a displaced person who offers herself to one of her husband's kin (Ruth 3); Bathsheba is presented as an object not a subject in the story of David using force to take and impregnate her (2 Samuel 11). The sexual dimensions of these ancestors' stories remind us that families are complicated and God's plans work themselves out in all sorts of ways. Scandals can't deter God's intentions to bless the world. Yet it's notable that the Bible doesn't depict these four women as dishonorable agents in their respective Old Testament stories. There's so much more to their histories than the prurient details that entice many interpreters. The legacies of these female branches in Jesus's family tree deserve more from us.

For one thing, Tamar, Rahab, and Ruth are all Gentiles, not born into the people of Israel. Bathsheba might also be a Gentile; we know that her husband, Uriah, whom David murders, is. The genealogical trajectories that culminate in the Messiah's arrival involve representatives from the wider world.

Moreover, the Gentile women in the genealogy also have a knack for demonstrating the true nature of faithfulness and obedience. Twice-widowed Tamar makes plain her father-in-law Judah's attempt to exploit her vulnerability through his selfish refusal to have his third son marry her, as the law demands. Rahab shows more faith in the God of Israel than do the fainthearted Hebrew spies hiding in her home. Ruth expresses unwavering loyalty to Naomi, her widowed Hebrew mother-in-law. Bathsheba in 1 Kings 1 plays a part in having

Solomon made king, but her motives for doing so are unclear and too knotty to untangle here.

As one of my teachers liked to say, "God has more stories," more than the Old Testament chooses to tell. These women's briefly told narratives assert that God's blessings travel widely, allowing all sorts of people to receive them and walk in God's righteousness. Matthew might tell the story of Jesus with a keen focus on how and why he matters for Jews and Judaism, but Matthew also signals to us that the whole world plays a part in God's plans. All are invited. Don't limit the guest list.

Matthew 9:9-13

(Mercy toward Matthew and His Ilk)

In all the Gospels, Jesus causes controversy for multiple reasons. Probably the habit that most upsets onlookers is his interest in embracing folks who appear to belong to the wrong crowd. I mean people whom the casual observer might not expect a religious leader to befriend, at least not without the leader first scolding them and making them change their pattern of living. But Jesus simply goes to these folks and forges social bonds with them by sharing space around dinner tables.

Of all the people Jesus calls to follow him, a man named Matthew may evoke the most surprise. As a Jew who makes his living collecting tolls from travelers and merchants on behalf of their Roman occupiers, Matthew undoubtedly attracts his neighbors' disdain. Some would regard him, whether fairly or not, as a collaborator who has chosen to betray his people and maybe his God.

I assume that the dinner that transpires later in the day happens in Matthew's home, as suggested in similar accounts in Mark 2:14-17 and Luke 5:27-32. The man called Matthew shows gratitude to Jesus and invites his friends to experience the same, so here come the local "tax collectors and sinners." We aren't told who the "sinners" are.

You might imagine a house full of moral degenerates, the worst of the worst, but the text is not so clear. Likely they didn't choose the name *sinners* for themselves. Perhaps they are indeed horrible people. Perhaps other people merely treat them that way or use the label *sinners* to mark them as outsiders, religiously apathetic, or people who reside beyond the social norms set up by the so-called honorable people. For whatever reason, this gathering doesn't measure up to the insiders' standards.

Jesus dines with people who, for whatever reasons, have exited, been left out of, or been thrown out of the religious and moral mainstream. It's easier to treat them without compassion if you dehumanize them with a word like sinners. Think of terms still used to diminish people as deviants or undeserving: thugs, felons, junkies, rednecks, *those* people.

As if by a powerful magnetic force, Jesus is drawn to people on society's edges, those who have lost a place at the community table, so to speak. He doesn't instruct them to change their behavior. He embraces them. In doing so he announces he doesn't intend "to call the righteous." That's not equivalent to rejecting more conventionally respectable people. His plan to remake the world is first and foremost an effort to lift up the ones who need a lift. Healthy people don't need his solidarity like "those who are sick" do. What's their sickness? It seems they've been left behind and not found a way back into the good graces of their community. What's his cure? He dignifies them by his presence and offers them a dose of divine mercy. They literally get a place at the table beside him.

It sometimes surprises people to discover that Jesus doesn't scold these "tax collectors and sinners." Although he begins his ministry in 4:17 urging people to "repent," he never says, "You there, quit working for the Romans" or "I know how much you've stolen from others, so cut it out." Rather he shares a table, implicitly pronouncing that his dinner companions belong to him, and he belongs to them. When he does single out specific sins for criticism in Matthew, it's to bemoan the hypocrisy of religious insiders. I'll discuss his displeasure with those leaders further in chapter 5.

Only Matthew's version of Jesus dining with this party of misfits explicitly refers to Hosea 6:6, where God declares, "I desire steadfast love and not sacrifice" (see again in Matthew 12:7). Those words don't imply, either in Hosea or in Matthew, that the Jewish sacrificial system and concerns about moral or ritual impurity mean nothing to God. Rather, the statement prioritizes mercy. Mercy is indispensable. Concern for legal and liturgical categories that aren't predicated on mercy don't interest Jesus. He wants people to recognize mercy at the heart of God's outlook on the world, and he wants them to treat one another accordingly.

The summons to follow Jesus goes out to people on both sides of the tracks, no matter who determines which side is the right or wrong one. But he himself chooses to spend his time on Matthew's side. Jesus voices no expectation that someone has to have their act together if they want to enjoy the benefits of life with him. Following him is a calling to embrace, or to be embraced by, his compassion, not a privilege reserved for people who purport to have the more respectable social résumé.

Matthew 11:28-30

(Easy Yoke, Light Burden)

If you're looking for a biblical passage to embroider and hang on your wall or to tattoo on your forearm (to each their own!), I recommend this one. I experience it like a glass of ice-cold water while working outdoors on a hot summer day. The statements Jesus makes here appear only in these verses and nowhere else in the Bible. Despite the difficult and occasionally harsh language Matthew serves us (like the "woe" Jesus pronounces on certain cities a few verses earlier, in 11:20-24), this passage makes me stick with Jesus and keep reading. I confess I'm more motivated by a carrot like this than by the stick of ominous warnings.

The passage speaks for itself quite well. Once again, Jesus shows his concern for people who need relief. He doesn't issue his invitation to folks with comfortable lives, but to those who live under "heavy burdens." Don't conclude that Jesus doesn't care about other people, but remember what he said back at the beginning of his first sermon (see chapter 1): he promises to go to those most in need of a blessing. That's his mission. His preference for downtrodden and weary people resides at the heart of his ministry.

Jesus asks his followers to wear a yoke, as an ox wears to harness its power while performing heavy labor. That may not seem an attractive metaphor for a life with Jesus, especially since in much of the Bible a yoke on a person symbolizes subjugation to someone else's usually oppressive will (for example, 1 Kings 12:6-11). Over time, however, Jewish teachers began to speak of a yoke also as an image for obedience to God, especially with regard to observing God's law. Jesus promises a restful experience with an "easy" yoke of obedience.

Obedience carries many negative connotations in our society. We teach dogs to obey. Disobedient children get disciplined or penalized. Obedience to Jesus, however, is a form of discipleship, a process of learning to walk in his way (see also 28:20, which we'll explore shortly). As you picture obedience, don't think about toeing the line to avoid punishment, but instead imagine what it means to imitate him. Or, as he says in this passage, we're talking about a process in which we "learn from" him. He's not our disciplinarian but our gentle teacher.

Matthew is a story about promised blessings, not earned wages.

In my own life, I don't often experience discipleship as "easy." Maybe I demand a perfectionism from myself that Jesus simply isn't requesting. After all, Matthew is a story about promised blessings, not earned wages. But sometimes I fall into the trap of assuming that discipleship entails excelling. I should reread 9:9-13, the story of the dinner party that Matthew the tax collector hosts for his friends and Jesus.

Since we're on the topic of my struggles, here's another one that I have in my own efforts toward discipleship: I often experience the way of Jesus as incredibly inconvenient. It asks me to surrender my own privileges and my sense of self-importance for the sake of the people whose loads need lightening. When I finally slow down, get over myself, and imagine Jesus present in the people who suffer "heavy burdens," however, I usually discover joy in discipleship.

Matthew 12:15-21

(Jesus's Appeal to the Crowds)

All four Gospels include summary statements, brief remarks like what we find in the first two verses of this passage. The summaries cause us to realize that the Gospel authors could have pulled many more stories out of the early churches' collective memories about Jesus and included them in their books. The longer stories we have—such as the series of passages describing Jesus healing a man stricken with paralysis, a woman suffering from chronic hemorrhaging, a girl who had just died, two men who cannot see, and a man who cannot speak (9:2-8, 18-34)—are detailed samples of a much more extensive body of work and not an exhaustive inventory of Jesus's actions.

The Gospels attempt to provide a character sketch of Jesus. They want to impress upon us what kind of person he was and what kinds of things he did. The Gospels are remarkably consistent insofar as they describe his ministry of healing and compassion. This particular passage contributes to Matthew's portrait of Jesus in two important ways: he is someone who appeals to and welcomes crowds, and his ministry corresponds to what Scripture promises.

First, crowds. Crowds are faceless characters in narratives as in real life. It can be difficult to distinguish individuals in a sea of humanity, which means it can be difficult to care about them. That's one reason why journalists try to get responses from individuals when there's an event affecting a mass of people. Anonymous swarms of folks often appear in connection to Jesus. They're drawn to him, as in this passage. They need healing, so they *follow* him, which is the primary action that disciples do.

The crowds' persistence says something about the magnitude of their needs and maybe also their desperation. We get the impression that Jesus circulates in a world eager for help. He doesn't need to seek out pain and suffering. Pain and suffering come to him, and he responds with healing. I imagine, based on the longer healing stories in Matthew, all of it happens not with a single wave of Jesus's hand but one person at a time, face-to-face.

His commitment to heal stems from his compassion. Although the word doesn't appear in this passage, on four separate occasions Matthew says, explicitly, that Jesus is moved to compassion for a crowd (9:36; 14:14; 15:32) or a pair of people (20:30–34).

The Greek verb for feeling compassion is delightful to know. Even my students who quickly forget what they learned in their Greek course usually remember it: *splagchnizomai*. It's fun to say out loud, if you want to give it a try. The word is built around the Greek noun *splagchna*, which means intestines or entrails. As you probably know, in American culture we refer to the head as the location of understanding and the heart as the seat of our will and emotions. In the ancient world, the bowels were associated with compassion. We might say that Jesus's compassion comes from the gut, maybe seizing his whole body the way that severe hunger might have your whole torso feeling tied in knots. Compassion is a visceral craving rumbling from deep within the Son of God.

Second, the promises of Scripture. The summary statement at the beginning of the passage we're exploring shares similarities with Mark 3:7-12, but Matthew is unique in that our passage concludes with a paraphrase of Isaiah 42:1-4. Matthew asserts that Jesus's ministry of compassion aligns with the testimony of Scripture. This is a common move in Matthew, for on at least twelve different occasions the action pauses and the narrator breaks in to say that an aspect of Jesus's story fulfills something God promised in previous generations. It's a feature of Matthew that makes this Gospel distinctive and reiterates that Jesus and his ministry stand fully in line with the Old Testament's perspectives on God.

In referring to Isaiah's statements about God's "servant," Matthew's point is not that Jesus alone is the person Isaiah has in mind. Rather, Jesus's humility and gentleness evoke memories of Isaiah, making that ancient passage true again. Or the Isaiah passage is true now in additional, expansive ways insofar as Matthew celebrates Jesus as God's servant. Through Jesus, God is doing something familiar, extending God's prior promises. This servant will transform the world. It will happen through his peaceful and nurturing ways, as indicated by the statements that the Gentiles (or "nations") will also benefit from him. Jesus won't raise an army or conquer with muscle. He tends to bruised bodies and smoldering souls. His ministry of restoration and compassion goes beyond being nice. Within it churns the power to change the world.

As we saw in chapter 3, Jesus calls his followers into the ministry he conducts. Assisting in the inbreaking of God's kingdom doesn't involve storming castles. It works to bring about healing and wholeness among people, especially those who have brittle souls or who reside in out-of-the-way places.

Matthew 15:29-31

(Crowds, Again)

Get ready for another summary statement. This particular one, worded as it is, appears only in Matthew. It therefore provides additional insight into Matthew's character sketch of Jesus. Once again, sizable crowds pursue Jesus. He heals a variety of people, and everyone responds with amazement.

In the Introduction, I discussed the notion of the "kingdom of heaven." Jesus anticipates the state of affairs that comes into being when God holds sway over the world, with God's desires for human flourishing coming into full, lived reality. Jesus talks about the Kingdom often, and many of his parables illustrate it, but here he expresses the Kingdom in his actions, even if the term itself doesn't appear in these verses.

By healing people, Jesus literally embodies the kingdom of God, allowing them to experience the wholeness, peace, and restoration that God promises the human family. I don't mean that the invitation to follow Jesus carries an implicit guarantee of wellness or prosperity. He never says that. Nonetheless, each healing allows us a moment to peer through the holes Jesus punches in the foundations of "the way things are." Each healing offers a taste of a transformed existence. Such stories call Jesus's disciples to prepare for the Kingdom's fullness to blossom by working to alleviate human suffering the best we can.

Healing stories can cause problems for at least two reasons, however. For one thing, they can create the impression that ailments and the handicaps that stem from them are indications of a person's moral or existential flaws. Even worse, these stories often lead people to associate conditions such as blindness and mobility challenges with sinfulness. Jesus heals people not because he wants to provide symbols about sin and forgiveness. He really yearns to alleviate human suffering when he encounters it. Alas, there's an endless supply of it. Ailments and limitations await everyone who ages. Jesus's healings in the Gospels don't last forever. People die. We should avoid interpreting Jesus's activity as an effort to "fix" people who are uniquely "broken."

The second problem arises when we suppose that Jesus heals people as a reward for their faith in him. Perhaps you've encountered faith healers or other preachers in real life or on television who promise healings in Jesus's name if only you believe *enough*. That can consign faithful Christians to suffer in a cloud of self-blame. It can also create twisted beliefs, as if someone who suffers must have displeased God. It's not as outlandish as it may sound. Many people who receive dire diagnoses often have to deal with folks asking whether they might have done anything sinful to cause their ailment. Tragically, somehow the church sometimes takes amazing healing stories like what we find in this passage and uses them to accuse or blame others who suffer.

This summary statement concludes by noting that the crowds offer praise to "the God of Israel." That detail contributes an additional reminder that Matthew presents Jesus as a Jew whose promised blessings stand squarely in line with the benevolent promises God makes in the Jewish scriptures (the Christian Old Testament). Jesus isn't calling people out of Judaism at all.

Matthew shows us Jews and Gentiles both opting to follow Jesus as the fulfillment of God's promises.

The reference to God in this scene as "the God of Israel" could also imply, ever so subtly, that these crowds around Jesus include Gentiles. Plenty of non-Jews lived in the region near the Sea of Galilee, so the notion of Gentiles drawn to this powerful healer isn't far-fetched. The Kingdom Jesus inaugurates extends to the nations, as well. As we saw in 12:15-21, where Matthew refers to Isaiah 42:1-4, Jesus attracts the nations. He does so by sheer virtue of his compassionate commitment to care for those in need. Matthew shows us Jews and Gentiles both opting to follow Jesus as the fulfillment of God's promises.

Matthew's story about Jesus, his magnetic appeal, and his disciples ministering with him is poised to expand. It's just waiting for Jesus to give the green light, which we'll see occur at the end.

Matthew 28:16-20

(The Great Commission)

Matthew tells a very Jewish story, in that the Gospel pays a lot of attention to Jesus's participation in first-century Jewish life. The story begins with a genealogy stretching back to Abraham and injects Jesus into lively debates about how Jews should interpret and observe God's law. Matthew keeps readers focused on the connections between Jesus's ministry and the testimony of Jewish scripture. Jesus directs his disciples to minister only to "the lost sheep of the house of Israel" (10:6; see also 15:24).

References to Gentiles nevertheless pop up every now and then, beginning even in the genealogy. Matthew simply can't tell an *exclusively* Jewish story, because Gentiles are in Jesus's lineage and they circulate in the places where he circulates. Dreamers have a way of drawing crowds everywhere.

Therefore, when this Gospel ends with the resurrected Jesus Christ commissioning his remaining disciples to "make disciples of all nations," and since the same Greek word can be translated either "nations" or "gentiles," it makes for a slightly predictable finale. At last it's crystal clear that Jesus and the Kingdom he manifests can't be contained or restricted. *Now* it's time to follow Jesus's trajectory in widening the scope. We go where Matthew has been pointing all along.

Jesus instructs some of his closest pupils—there are others, including a number of women, as we learn in 27:55-56—to open the door to additional pupils. Jesus doesn't send them *away* from their Jewish friends and neighbors, as if he's turning his back on Judaism or starting a new, different religion. He expands the circle. Jesus doesn't commission his followers to raise an army or colonize the world. He wants additional communities to "obey" him, which we know is a form of imitating him. Specifically, he wants people to obey his teachings, which will unleash more mercy in the world. Maximizing mercy is the church's mission.

The disciples go out under Jesus's "authority." They possess not their own authority, but his. That authority shows itself as he teaches and reveals God's kingdom (see 7:29, where the word *authority* first appears). Disciples do the things he does and pass along his message, both what he has spoken and what he has enacted. Moreover, Jesus's disciples take up his work as people empowered by his enduring presence. Even today, Jesus remains. We should still refer to him as Emmanuel, which means "God is with us," as Matthew tells us in its first chapter (1:23).

What's the most beautiful thing about these disciples whom Jesus sends to continue transforming the world? They're far from perfect. That is, their faith remains incomplete. Matthew tells us, "They worshiped him, but they doubted" (28:17). Their double-mindedness makes sense, given that the Resurrection happened just a few verses prior to this scene. They're living a contradiction, it seems, at least in their outlook toward Jesus. He commissions them anyway. They—like all disciples—will remain a work in progress. So will the church.

In a Gospel that occasionally portrays Jesus as breathing fire and warning people of a coming judgment, there's great relief in seeing some of Jesus's closest followers going forward while still harboring doubts. Doubt isn't necessarily the enemy of faith. Sometimes it hones faith and makes it adapt. Doubt doesn't disqualify you from being Jesus's disciple.

Reflections

Our understanding of discipleship needs to begin with what Jesus does, not what we do. I've observed people getting derailed by worrying too much about what they need to do or—even worse—what other Christians need to be doing. We sometimes envision discipleship as if it's a portfolio we must build, showing our progress in a number of areas like worship attendance, service projects, financial stewardship, and Bible study. Those are all useful, but Jesus's main imperative to people is "follow." It's not "grow," "diversify," "shape up," or "work harder." He sets the agenda. He inaugurates the kingdom of God. He promises to move us forward and accompany us.

The passages we've explored illustrate that following Jesus entails joining him on a path or a way of life characterized by a welcoming embrace and extravagant mercy. Openness to others and generous compassion can express themselves in a variety of ways, depending on who you are, where you live, and what resources you have available to you. But those dispositions constitute the core of what all disciples do.

What would it take for us, as Jesus's followers, to be known for our mercy, not our squabbles, condescension, or self-protectiveness?

The needs of the world sometimes strike us as so massive, and our ability to follow Jesus often feels so wobbly, we don't know where to begin. I expect he'd tell us to begin with mercy. And end with it. We noted that Jesus refers to Hosea 6:6, where God expresses a desire for mercy over sacrifice. I imagine Jesus telling congregations in our time, whether they feel sturdy or shaky, "I desire mercy over preserving your reputation." To leaders he might say, "I desire mercy, not ambition." To communities that are stuck, "I desire mercy, not strategy sessions and rebranding efforts." To people too hard on themselves and others, "I desire mercy, not shaming." To all of his disciples, "I desire mercy, not power." At least he's consistent, always pointing the way with mercy as his North Star. What would it take for us, as Jesus's followers, to be known for our mercy, not our squabbles, condescension, or self-protectiveness?

When Jesus calls others to gather around him and follow, we rarely observe him interacting with a disciple one-on-one. He's surrounded by a group—a community. Americans in particular like to think of ourselves as individually defined, but Matthew's account of Jesus's interactions with people indicate that following Jesus is a collective, cooperative endeavor. What does mercy look like as a communal effort? How does a group of disciples represent Jesus with both worship and doubt woven among themselves? We walk this path together, as part of the whole ragtag crew Jesus calls to himself.

Chapter 5

Conflicts and Criticisms

Passages to Explore:

Matthew 23:1-36	(Blistering Attacks on Scribes and Pharisees)
Matthew 25:1-13	(Wise and Foolish Bridesmaids)
Matthew 25:14-30	(A Buried Talent)
Matthew 27:11-26	(Pilate's Cunning and Cruelty)
Matthew 27:62–28:6	(Guards at the Tomb)

To put it bluntly: if you're recounting a story about a guy who's crucified, the story is obviously about conflict. The Romans crucified people for sedition or undermining public order, so Jesus's ministry involved more than spreading love and warmth. It's a hard-edged story. As we already observed in chapter 2, Jesus's appearance in the world signals a coming reckoning, since Jesus has truth to reveal. Not everyone likes to hear the truth. But apparently that's part of what it takes for Jesus's vision for new life to emerge.

To understand any Gospel we need to dig into the conflicts that surround Jesus and his ministry. Since we're called to share in his ministry, we need to know what its flash points are and why they exist. Misunderstanding those details can yield harmful results. We must handle the passages we're about to explore with care.

In all the Gospels, the devil (sometimes called Satan) is Jesus's main yet unseen adversary. Matthew describes the devil's attempts to lure Jesus into embracing counterfeit forms of power and influence (4:1-11). Jesus nevertheless talks infrequently about the devil, so I follow his example. I get wary when people blame devils for everything. I'm more worried about the chaos and oppression that humanity creates on its own. In this chapter we'll explore instances where Matthew indicates that people create problems. There are some specific problems that Jesus goes out of his way to identify and denounce.

When influential people misbehave, others get hurt.

The people he criticizes the most hold power or responsibility in religious and political contexts. He's concerned with people who can influence how others live. He has little sympathy for religious and political leaders who misuse their authority and distort what God desires for humanity. When influential people misbehave, others get hurt.

Especially in Matthew, Jesus detests religious devotion that turns hypocritical, lethargic, misdirected, or just somehow genuinely unconcerned with other people's well-being. The annoyance comes out in the accusations he hurls at certain religious leaders, in parables warning his followers against becoming callous, and in the Gospel's depiction of the Roman Empire's arrogant misuse of power. The criticisms that are most severe and most frequent in Matthew mean to reconfirm God's determination to bring about the kingdom of heaven. Jesus calls out—

both explicitly and implicitly—actions and assumptions that could keep people from encountering the fullness and justice God desires.

Matthew 23:1-36
(Blistering Attacks on Scribes and Pharisees)

As they do in all the Gospels, Pharisees and other Jewish authorities in Matthew voice concerns about Jesus and his movement (for example, 9:11; 15:1-2). They wonder, sometimes disapprovingly, why he seems uninterested in certain practices that they embrace.

As he does in all the Gospels, Jesus criticizes groups of Pharisees in Matthew. He chastises them for the hypocrisy he perceives in them. Matthew distinguishes itself from the other Gospels, however, through the ferocity of those criticisms and through amplifying accusations toward Pharisees in particular. As I mentioned in the Introduction, this Gospel depicts Jesus as eager to discredit other Jewish teachers. His most vicious attacks on Pharisees and their associates, the scribes, appear in this passage. He refers to both groups as a "brood of vipers" (v. 33). He calls them accomplices in the murder of God's prophets over the generations, which makes them fit for punishment in the vileness and misery of *Gehenna* (vv. 29-35). Most of all, he believes they, as religious leaders, pose a danger to others because of how they neglect mercy and obstruct people from the kingdom of heaven. To him they are "blind guides" (v. 16), "blind fools" (v. 17), and "hypocrites" who look attractive on the outside but corrupt the world with the pollution that hides inside (v. 27). On a different occasion he calls a group of Pharisees "evil" (12:34).

This passage should disturb us, even on a first reading, because these religious leaders sing only one note in Matthew. Maybe it reminds you of times when your mean and bigoted relative (whom you can't bring yourself to unfollow) starts a social-media post with the phrase *The problem with Italians is...* or *How come Catholics always...* In other words, Matthew's depiction of scribes and Pharisees in general is absolutely negative. They don't get to speak for themselves. Should we really believe that all of them were entirely horrible people who didn't have any good ideas or redeeming qualities? Every now and then the other three Gospels portray individual scribes and Pharisees a little more charitably. In Matthew, however, they all appear as one-dimensional, sensationalized caricatures.

Instead of walking through this challenging passage and commenting on each part, it's more fruitful to ponder both why Matthew includes such stiff rebukes from Jesus's mouth and how Christians can respond today.

The author of Matthew might have chosen to leave room for an additional chapter or two containing stories about Jesus healing people, assuming that those stories would be worth passing along to believers. But the author elected to include this passage instead. Evidently the author thought that a sharp reproof of the Pharisees and scribes would be more useful to the Gospel's audiences. In other words, we can assume the author had motives for including stories about Jesus blasting other religious teachers.

Who were those teachers? Scribes interpreted Jewish law and taught folks how to observe it in their daily lives. Not all Pharisees had the credentials the scribes had as legal experts. Pharisees were mostly laypeople who had more "normal" jobs. Pharisees, like most of the trained scribes, nevertheless committed themselves to observing Torah in aspects of their ordinary tasks and responsibilities. Pharisees believed that law observance was about more than priestly rituals and visits to the Jerusalem Temple; it extended to how Jews conduct their regular affairs with high regard for honoring God's holiness. They valued accumulated wisdom about how various laws should correspond to specific circumstances, such as ritualized handwashing before meals. Law obedience didn't impose an unfair, harsh burden on them, for they considered God's law a source of blessing. They didn't devote themselves to Torah to earn their own salvation or produce what Christians still derisively (and mistakenly) call "works righteousness." They believed in God's grace and willingness to forgive, as Christians do.

Once Roman soldiers destroyed the Jerusalem Temple in 70 CE, Pharisees and certain groups of scribes rose in prominence within Judaism. Their teachings about honoring God's holiness in Jewish homes, communities, and workplaces made it possible for people to live according to Jewish values and convictions even without the benefit of temple-based practices, which had become impossible. Judaism adapted, thanks greatly to the descendants of scribes and Pharisees who survived the temple's decimation in 70. Still today, different Jewish "denominations" are heirs of the "Rabbinic Judaism" that emerged during about the same period when Christianity was defining itself.

Matthew appears bent on discrediting scribes and Pharisees as part of its attempt to lift up Jesus. Matthew was written when Rabbinic Judaism was beginning to take shape in the decades after the temple. It's easy to imagine why the author might have wanted readers to consider Jesus as the preeminent interpreter of the law. Different Jewish groups, including groups of Jews who followed Jesus, were insisting they knew the best directions that Jewish ideas and practices pointed. Stories about Jesus rebuking scribes and Pharisees caught the author's attention. Those episodes make Jesus look good while stripping his rivals of their credibility. In the Introduction I mentioned that Matthew shows evidence that believers were looking to some of Jesus's teachings to help them navigate grudges, rivalries, and suspicions during a formative time. Those kinds of tensions threaten to fray and snap when groups can't agree about which teachers to trust or what belief systems to adopt. I'm not defending Matthew's belligerent caricature of Pharisees and scribes; I'm explaining its power for influencing Matthew's ancient readers.

If I were to walk you through hundreds of pages of detailed scholarly analysis, two things would happen. One: you'd be glad when I'm done. Two: you'd discover that no one can declare with certainty whether Jesus really said all of this to any Pharisees and scribes with such an unyielding punch. If he really did, I hope he'd be mortified to know someone wrote it down. Whether he really did or didn't, in either case the author of Matthew was grinding an ax by including this material and angrily fashioning it as such a one-sided portrait of these Jewish leaders.

Even without reviewing scholarly analysis, I can offer you good guesses about why the author of Matthew chose to include anti-Pharisee invective so prominently in the Gospel. Most likely it's part of a strategy to bind Christian communities tightly to Jesus. It's to guard Christian communities from Jewish teachers and groups that had rocky relationships with those who believed in Jesus Christ. Lingering trauma from schism or estrangement could have had something to do with it. We can't recover the exact reasons why those relationships deteriorated.

The specific history behind the exaggerated reprimands of scribes and Pharisees remains murky, but there's something I can tell you with much more certainty: it's wrong for Christians (or anyone else) to espouse or repeat what the passage says.

The criticism Jesus speaks in this passage must not be used as a blanket criticism of Judaism and Jews, past or present. The passage has been used that way over the centuries. For one thing, Matthew doesn't present Jesus's criticisms for that purpose. It's not a passage that seeks to contrast "the Christian way" (if there even was a single such thing) with "the Jewish way" (again, as if there was only one). We should acknowledge that the passage isn't an accurate characterization of what law obedience must be about. What it delivers is a criticism of hypocrisy and inattentiveness to the charity and compassion that God desires. That's what should most impress itself on we Christians who read it. To treat hypocrisy as a distinctively Jewish failing is a deplorable move and a misunderstanding of Jesus's own participation in ancient Jewish debates about life and the law.

I'm belaboring the point because when someone grumbles that their sanctimonious coworker is "such a Pharisee," they're reinforcing a long-standing antisemitic stereotype. Christians (and anyone else) can't insinuate that Jewish law obedience (which the Pharisees championed) somehow always winds up in dishonest religion or sham holiness. That's a hateful claim, in and of itself. This is a vital concern, given the terrible history of anti-Judaism in the Christian church and the recent proliferation of antisemitic incidents in the USA. We have to consider how this passage reflects the ancient worry and anger lurking in Matthew—not so we can pretend the passage doesn't matter anymore, but so we can stop tearing down Judaism to prop up Christianity.

How should we respond to this passage? First, let it remind us about ancient history. Jesus taught and ministered during a time when people had conflicting ideas about how to live as Jews in an occupied land. In the Gospels he expresses his displeasure when he thinks certain teachings and priorities among his contemporaries neglect "the weightier matters of the law: justice and mercy and faith" (v. 23). He also surely made common cause with some of his fellow Jewish religious authorities, even if that detail gets no attention in Matthew.

To use Jesus to demean Judaism is both wrong and malicious.

Second, remember that Jesus was Jewish and never set about to lose his religion. In Matthew he has critical things to say about how certain folks interpret and adhere to the law, but he never disparages someone simply for having high regard for Torah. He himself is a big fan. He praises Torah's greatest commandments (22:34-40). His own teachings draw from the law to communicate his vision for the world (5:17–6:1), as you'll recall from chapter 3. To use Jesus to demean Judaism is both wrong and malicious.

Third, we do well to confess openly that Christians too often take passages like this one to turn Judaism—and, by extension, Jewish people—into a piñata. The church's history should prompt us to repent of anti-Judaism (denigration of Jews and Judaism for theological motives) and its modern product, antisemitism (a form of racism against Jewish people). Let's commit ourselves to correcting misperceptions and repairing the damage.

Fourth, we ought to take Jesus's anger about hypocrisy seriously, even as we protest any insinuation that all Pharisees and scribes were deceitful hypocrites. I'm susceptible to hypocrisy and I suppose you are too. Jesus criticizes the Pharisees in this passage, but not because he despises them. He despises hypocrisy and religious patterns that keep people walled off from the mercy and rest that God provides. Were ancient Pharisees capable of committing mistakes like that? It's fair to assume that once in a while some were. Was hypocrisy what all the Pharisees were entirely about? Of course not. The better question to consider is: when, how, and why are you and I capable of those errors?

Jesus has expectations for the people he calls to himself. He knows we're capable of obstructing his promised blessings, so this passage warns us—in both indirect and problematic ways—to examine ourselves and use our privileges for the sake of God's kingdom.

Matthew 25:1-13

(Wise and Foolish Bridesmaids)

Matthew 25:14-30

(A Buried Talent)

These two parables aren't exactly the same, but since both make similar points it's helpful to examine them together. Both reiterate Jesus's frustrations toward religious people who hinder others' access to God's blessings. Both have disturbing endings. This time he's not upset with Pharisees and scribes. He's warning his own followers to avoid falling into carelessness and negligence. He wants them to live in ways that will make a difference in the world.

The parables sit in the midst of Jesus's final extended speech, which covers Matthew 24–25. The speech prepares his followers to live until the time when the kingdom of heaven arrives in all its fullness. He sketches a grim landscape marked by wars, natural disasters, persecution, and deceptive leaders—an era when love "will grow cold" (24:3-14). That sounds too familiar. He describes perilous conditions for anyone who is "poor in spirit" or limping along with "little faith." It's hardly a time for Jesus's followers to be stingy with mercy or unaware of the privileges they enjoy. Jesus's death and resurrection clearly don't transform the world into a safe or kind place. The struggle continues.

Christianity is a waiting religion. We wait for the complete arrival of the Kingdom. We don't wish for the end of time, but we long for a new quality of living. Waiting is difficult work. It's active work. Taxing work. We can tear our communities apart in the process if we aren't careful. We can trade Jesus's values for weak substitutes.

Both parables speak about distinctions emerging among religious insiders who have to wait. The parables don't describe the overall population but people entrusted to do special things. Some of the insiders wait well, while the stress of waiting and bearing responsibilities makes others overwhelmed, uncaring, anesthetized, or cowardly. In the first parable all ten young women, or bridesmaids, appear the same. They all have the same function. They all want to meet the groom. They were invited. They wait through the night. They fall asleep.

When the time comes to light lamps, we discover who's foolish—the ones who weren't ready to wait an extended time. They took their responsibility too casually and didn't anticipate the contingencies they might have to negotiate. Evidently all ten had resources they could have used to procure enough oil, but half didn't do so. I admit that this detail drives me crazy because I'm a person who gets very frustrated when I have to wait for people who are late…I mean really late. (What's up with this groom?) In the parable, though, the groom's delay doesn't absolve the women of their responsibilities as illuminators. We can presume they know that the wedding's starting time might be flexible.

In the second parable, three enslaved men receive authority to manage someone's fortune while he's away. Although they receive different amounts, all have the same role. Two do their job, but one refuses. It's a difficult scenario from a modern perspective. Ancient teachers often used stories of wealthy people who entrust things to their subordinates as a test of their character, but many of us rightly balk at viewing our relationship with God as similar to enslavement to someone who controls us. Reading the Bible always leads us into different cultural terrain. We need to understand that terrain if we're to comprehend the parable's main concerns.

The enslaved men receive talents. This doesn't mean they learn how to juggle or play the harmonica. Remember from chapter 3 that a talent was a monetary unit, about thirty pounds of gold or fifteen years of income for a laborer. Just one talent equals a stunning amount to delegate to an enslaved person, so the parable underscores the magnificent extent of the privilege and influence the master bestows on the three men. But one of them chooses not to embrace the opportunity. He squanders a tremendous gift and takes for granted his chance to advance his master's project.

I've heard people treat these parables as simple morality tales, like graduation speeches urging students to persevere through hardships and to take brave risks in life. Don't let anyone make these parables so dull. In addition, don't assume that the first parable asks us to hoard resources. The second one shouldn't lead us to idolize economic growth or accuse people of laziness when they can't make a decent living. These parables are emphasizing the grand blessings Jesus gives his followers to spread around.

The blessings Jesus provides aren't about status or money; Matthew doesn't preach a prosperity gospel. They're about the joy of an invitation to a lavish banquet and the delight of extending the

Kingdom's precious mercy. Jesus doesn't explicitly dissect the parables for us, but the only way I can make sense of the urgency and the harsh outcomes in both of them is to suppose that he's asking his followers not to give up on our calling to use our energy and our influence to do the things Jesus does. As I said, when influential people misbehave, others get hurt.

He abhors it when religious piety (or the utter lack of it) ends up harming people. As we saw in chapter 3, Jesus is determined that his flock not lose track of anyone. He warns the church not to deteriorate as it waits and not to become self-satisfied. Jesus pours out abundant blessings. We sometimes act instead as if we can afford to offer only scarcity.

What would faithful waiting look like, according to Matthew's overall narrative? What would happen if those women had more oil and the third man did something with the talent? Everyone will fall asleep from time to time, but we wake up to advocate for those who need solidarity. We embody the kingdom of heaven. We seek reconciliation with others. We relieve burdens. We sustain our neighbors when they struggle. We hold each other up when doubt and exhaustion become acute. We refuse to view mercy as a chore.

The punishments at the end of both parables seem excessive. I can't make them palatable, so I conclude they're meant to get our attention. Maybe they're hyperbole. In any case, they lead me to conclude that Jesus is so committed to providing blessings to the world that it utterly exasperates him when his followers refuse their callings to announce good news and to stand against lies, oppression, and fake spirituality. When religious faith makes us presume that our calling to join with Jesus is a privilege we can bury in the face of a hurting world, something has gone very wrong.

Before you worry that you're the third guy who sticks his talent in a hole and you're due for a smiting, consider also that the parables might lead us to recognize the corporate aspects of Christian faith. How do groups express faith? Sometimes congregations manage to prove generally faithful to their callings. Sometimes they're so worried about self-survival that they neglect compassion. These parables might provide a wake-up call to the ways in which faith communities can lose track of their priorities. No one is always faithful. Some of our efforts are misguided; some aren't. Beware again of strict dualisms.

Matthew 27:11-26
(Pilate's Cunning and Cruelty)

In at least two ways we've been trained to read Pilate incorrectly, especially Matthew's depiction of him.

First, a popular view of Pilate assumes him to be weak-willed, as if he's caught between a desire to free an innocent man and the roar of a crowd demanding a crucifixion. Too many cinematic portraits and melodramatic actors in passion plays have turned Pilate into a failed antihero, as if he's a Roman Prince Hamlet who knows the right thing to do but lacks the backbone. Ancient readers who remembered Pilate, who ruled Judea at the Roman emperor's behest from 26 to 36 CE, would assess him differently. He was known to be rash, hardly committed to fairness, and overly eager to provoke his Jewish subjects. In fact, he was eventually removed from office because of his heavy-handed approaches.

Second, people sometimes assume that Jesus's case presents Pilate with a legal dilemma. Indeed, Luke's version of the story may suggest this, but Matthew's doesn't. A Roman prefect like Pilate wasn't supposed to weigh evidence in light of an abstract legal code. For the most part, the prefect himself was the law. His responsibility was to uphold the sovereign authority of the Roman emperor. If someone of low social status claimed to be the inaugurator of a different kingdom led by a different king, the hearing would end about as soon as it began. Pilate has virtually no choice but to crucify someone like Jesus.

From a legal point of view, Pilate doesn't need to worry about violating Jesus's rights. From a political point of view, he has to execute someone acclaimed to be a king, especially if the local elites aren't objecting. He takes his time with Jesus during the hearing because he has more to gain from the moment than simply ridding the empire of yet another nuisance who's undercutting the idea of Roman supremacy. He has an empire to protect. Matthew's depiction of Pilate spotlights the prefect's deviousness. Jesus is executed by a sly, tyrannical system that knows how to keep its foot on the necks of the population it controls.

Jesus is executed by a sly, tyrannical system that knows how to keep its foot on the necks of the population it controls.

When Pilate briefly questions Jesus, Jesus stands before him bound (27:2) and beaten (27:27-31). Imagine Pilate's initial question, *"Are you the king of the Jews?"* (v. 11) voiced in a tone flooded with sarcasm. *Really? You? You look pathetic. You're supposed to be a king, yet your own people did this to you? Maybe you're the kind of king the Jewish people deserve!*

Pilate ignores a message from his wife, warning him to leave Jesus alone. At the beginning of Jesus's life, divine messages in dreams give Joseph guidance (1:20-21; 2:19-20). They also keep Jesus safe from Herod (2:12-13). A dream might have saved Jesus again, here in Jerusalem, but Pilate won't listen. He has a job to perform, and he relishes it.

When Pilate questions the crowd—a crowd that has been influenced by Jerusalem's chief priests and elders—it's more interrogation than survey. When he asks what he should do with the man called the Messiah, he certainly isn't letting the crowd test-drive his emperor-given authority to decide the fate of someone who proclaims a different kingdom. Read his question like this, "All of you know what happens to messiahs around here... don't you?" He extracts from the crowd something like a pledge of their loyalty to Rome's way. In the process he makes it plain that he's only doing his duty, and he reminds the crowd of the futility of expecting a deliverer to save them—not while Rome is in charge. The crowd grows agitated.

The manipulation continues through a ritual that only Matthew includes. Pilate washes his hands and shifts blame to the crowd. At least, he announces that shift. He knows he's in charge of the situation. He's not off-loading responsibility as much as he's subtly pulling everyone else into it. It's the art of a tyrant.

By washing his hands, Pilate recalls a ritual prescribed in Deuteronomy 21:1-9, which means to protect a city from bad consequences following an unsolved murder. In appropriating the ritual for a different setting, Pilate purports to be doing what he must do to protect Judea and its people in the future. He's implying he's not to blame for what's coming next; he's just carrying out his responsibility for the good of all. The crowd responds with a shocking claim, "His blood be on us and on our children!" (v. 25). The crowd has become like its leaders—both the priestly elites who demand Jesus's death and the Roman governor who's charged with reasserting Roman dominance. Pilate manipulates the crowd into complicity for the violence about to be done to Jesus the Messiah.

We need to pause and note that the crowd's final claim has been interpreted in sinister ways throughout Christian history. Some have taken this verse (v. 25) to support the awful idea that Jewish people of all times and places bear responsibility for killing Jesus. It matters little whether Matthew means the verse to imply such a thing, because those interpretations have already done their damage. They have claimed a kind of biblical approval for violence against Jews. I'll return to this verse in chapter 6, in hopes that it might point us toward new and generous ways of repairing mistakes made in the past.

Some dangerous authorities are lazy. Some are inept. Pilate is evasive, for he minimizes his own role in the evil that transpires and pins the blame on others. There's an abusive psychology at work that manages to destroy Jesus and debase anyone who would side with him and the Kingdom he inaugurates. Pilate provides a model for how domineering people thrive when they lure others into shouldering blame for the abuses they commit.

Pilate engineers the moment and eclipses the truth masterfully, but what does that mean for our view of Jesus and his crucifixion? As Matthew depicts it, Jesus dies in a world harassed by predatory leadership. Pilate embodies the layers of untrustworthiness residing in leaders and systems that oppress people, whether it's in the suffering that people have to endure, the hardships that never recede, the heavy burdens that folks must carry, or the labels that people are forced to wear. The kingdom of heaven stands against those realities, offering something better. But the old kingdoms of this world refuse to loosen their grip. Their hold on power makes it difficult to hope that Jesus's vision for the world can materialize. Those kingdoms presume to have the last word in their efforts to squelch Jesus and the blessings he promises. Come Sunday, however, a new last word will ring out.

Matthew 27:62–28:6

(Guards at the Tomb)

Many of us know the Easter story: Joseph of Arimathea places Jesus's corpse in a tomb on Friday, and a group of women discover the tomb empty around sunrise on Sunday morning, after the Jewish Sabbath has passed. All four Gospels include those basic details, with one minor exception (John mentions not a group of women but only Mary Magdalene). Although Matthew follows the basic script, it also says more, telling us that Jewish leaders persuade Pilate to provide soldiers to guard the tomb. They fear that disciples of the crucified "imposter" will steal his body and falsely claim a resurrection. For good measure, they seal the stone in place, covering and effectively locking the mouth of the cave.

By including this story of a fortified tomb, Matthew equips its earliest readers to rebut accusations from Jews outside of the church—

maybe specifically from Pharisees—that Jesus's resurrection was a hoax (see also 28:11-15). It's another example of this Gospel's troubling tendency to chastise Jews in a general sense for not embracing Jesus. At the same time, Matthew sets us up to experience the power of Easter in a particular way. In the other three Gospels the discovery of an open and empty tomb accentuates the mystery of Easter. Breaking open a sealed and guarded tomb with witnesses present makes Matthew's resurrection story a display of divine power.

Matthew's version would be the most fun to re-create if we were making a blockbuster film with a vast special-effects budget. "Mary Magdalene and the other Mary" witness (and feel) an earthquake. Then an angel—blessed with a powerlifter's physique, in my imagination—rolls away the stone and sits on it for good measure. It's the equivalent of a home run hitter dramatically flipping the bat before trotting to first base. The terrified soldiers become catatonic before the angel makes the resurrection announcement to the Marys. It's all big, loud, decisive, and powerful. The greatest fighting force in the world at the time, which is represented by paralyzed Roman soldiers flat on the ground, won't have the last word about Jesus after all.

For Matthew, the resurrection of Jesus Christ doesn't mean a declaration of war against Rome in particular or imperial authority in general. It nevertheless rebukes "the way things are." It boldly announces God's power to remake the world and institute a new "normal," one defined by God's rule ("the kingdom of heaven"). The earthquake symbolizes God's presence and a cosmic transformation about to begin, as if a hotrod is revving its engines at the starting line. Not even death will separate people from God or from God's blessings, for the power of resurrection is about more than extended life or a second chance at life. It's about a new quality of life with God.

The power over Roman authority, soldiers, and weapons likewise celebrates God's strength over the guile and cynicism of Pilate. Pilate simply does his job, so to speak, but his job entails resisting and suppressing God's kingdom. All of us can be guilty of the same, whether we lead prominent institutions or just survive from day to day on our own. The power of the Resurrection tells us that God can break those patterns of resistance—not by doing violence to us but by freeing us from our habits of abetting our societies' dogged attempts to obstruct God's kingdom.

Reflections

Jesus lived and ministered in a climate of conflict, some of which he initiated. Matthew likewise emerged within a conflicted environment. But this isn't a story merely about past struggles. Some of Matthew's acidic criticisms of hypocrisy, religious indifference, and political rackets still resonate today. They prompt us to consider how we avoid the hazards that often ensnare religious people. The topics of this chapter highlight the value of returning regularly to the beginning of the Sermon on the Mount (5:1-12) and Jesus's assurance that he provides rest for people's souls (11:28-30). He has blessings to promise to new generations.

Jesus lived and ministered in a climate of conflict, some of which he initiated.

The conflicts and criticisms we encounter in Matthew all come out of ancient historical realities, whether those relate to tensions and hostilities within ancient religious communities, worries about believers' ability to persist in their callings as Jesus's disciples, or the menace caused by imperial arrogance. Those realities still exist, of course, but now in different forms of distress, bitterness, uneasiness, and arrogance. I worry about oppressive teachings, persistent antisemitism, complacent spirituality, and abusive leadership all the time. That's mostly because I experience them so often—in the stories people tell me about their traumatizing experiences in toxic congregations, in the difficult church systems that I watch seminary students and graduates navigate, in the latest ridiculous thing that some Christian from somewhere wrote on the internet, and in the fact that poverty, suffering, and racism still run rampant in communities where significant numbers of people go to church and identify as Christians. Why are God's blessings so slow to arrive?

Jesus still speaks through Matthew, if we listen attentively and take seriously his desire to enlist us in his merciful work. We'll revisit these topics from a different angle in chapter 6. I think Matthew has more to offer us beyond stern criticisms and warnings about the urgency of God's kingdom, the high stakes of Jesus's message, and our propensity to stumble. We'll find plenty of constructive advice for our faith as well.

Taking Matthew Seriously Today

Passages to Explore:

Matthew 2:1-12	(Magi from the East)
Matthew 13:24-30, 36-43	(Weeds Interspersed among Wheat)
Matthew 13:31-32	(From Mustard Seed to Tree)
Matthew 27:25	(The Stain of Bloodguilt)

This entire book has aimed to take Matthew seriously. I've attempted to lead us into Matthew's landscape, not like a tour guide showing you where you can take interesting selfies in front of foreign and curious ruins from the past, but like a cultural interpreter helping you absorb and respond to Matthew by paying attention to this Gospel's ways of talking about Jesus and the world. What makes this chapter any different?

This chapter's approach won't diverge drastically from what you've already read. I simply want to highlight some aspects of Matthew that strike me as especially worth our attention now, given how I experience our current place and time.

I'm fully aware that "our current place and time" is impossible to capture. We inhabit many different places and times. I don't claim to speak for all Christians. I don't even claim to speak for all Christians who look like me or who possess the advantages I enjoy. I'm going to try to draw the circle wide enough that you can either find your place within it or imaginatively adjust the circle yourself so it encompasses your situation and concerns.

I'll be honest: I find Matthew a challenging Gospel. You might have guessed, as early as the Introduction, that the anger and intensity that occasionally growl through Matthew's pages concern me. I'm also troubled by Christians who soak up the Gospel's heat and redirect it toward other people like it's a weapon. It's dangerous to treat Matthew as a bag full of threats to pick out and lob at the world. I reject the impulse to treat Matthew as a license for churches to turn wrathful or arrogant when people disregard their message.

I reject the impulse to treat Matthew as a license for churches to turn wrathful or arrogant when people disregard their message.

In recent years, however, I've started to appreciate Matthew as a stimulating conversation partner. I'm not looking to adopt its anger but to grapple with the irritation and alarm that reside behind it. In part, that's because I've tried to acknowledge my own propensity for anger and disappointment—directed not toward the world "out there" but toward the Christian church in general. I watch in horror as the narratives and resentments of white Christian nationalism make gains in my country. I receive news from pastors about congregations sliding into the mire of snippy polarization. Church people, when they become stiff-necked, tend to imitate the broader culture in being quick to stop communicating about hard topics and eager to stay barricaded in isolated groups. I read strident articles from Christians who never bother to question whether their convictions might be wrong, hurtful, or too small. I witness love growing cold (to borrow an expression from Matthew 24:12) in our national politics and even in congregations, leaving displaced and disenfranchised people vulnerable, persecuted people unprotected, and economically or psychologically challenged people alone to fend for themselves in a society that treats them as expendable.

How did we reach a point where preachers who speak about the church's calling to support refugees with generosity and welcome are criticized for being "too political"? Why are some predominantly white congregations unwilling to talk about the corrosive effects of racism and how it manifests itself in national policies and theological traditions? Why does the church often seem preoccupied with devoting massive time and resources to strategizing about how to update its structures and programs, when Jesus declares over and over that his concern is to deliver mercy to unmerciful places and to heal divisions through reconciliation?

My frustrations take me in two directions. Sometimes I want to write others off. I want to say to other professed Christians, "We obviously don't believe in the same God." (There's my frustration popping up: I tend to call them "professed Christians" instead of "Christians.") I want to lash out and pretend I'm authorized to declare stern consequences like Jesus does from time to time.

At other times I want to withdraw into complacency because the struggle feels too exhausting.

For some reason, Matthew speaks to me in those frustrated moments. I draw inspiration from the intensity with which Matthew talks about mercy and the church's capacity to carry on Jesus's work in the world. Matthew shakes me up because it reminds me that people, maybe especially in religious communities, are prone to inflict wounds on themselves when they grow too preoccupied with blaming other people. This Gospel knows how good we are at burying talents and caricaturing others.

As we've discussed, Matthew evidently was written during a time when religious people disagreed sharply with each other, making folks agitated. At the same time, Matthew wants believers not to become distracted by their quarrels to the point where they stop living out Jesus's good news of mercy and grace. Even as Matthew warns of great risks, still it considers the tasks aligned with God's kingdom as easy to summarize and therefore hard to ignore. What are those tasks? They summon us to join Jesus in showing mercy and acceptance. What might that look like today, especially with all the distractions around us?

Matthew 2:1-12

(Magi from the East)

Few things can rattle your quiet sense of order like the unannounced arrival of visitors. When strangers show up to visit Jesus after his birth, they bring more than the gifts we sing about in the hymn "We Three Kings." They bring surprise, insight, new perspective, partnerships, and courage. Their sheer presence shocks us, beckoning us to break free from our tendencies toward insular thinking.

I occasionally ask students to imagine they're responsible for adapting a story from the Gospels into a film. Which Hollywood A-lister should portray Mary Magdalene? What music will play during the Transfiguration? How many people do you think witness Jesus's triumphal entry into Jerusalem, and what's the difference between a crowd of two dozen and one of two thousand? I want students to examine how and why their perspectives on an event have already been shaped. It's important for them to consider what mood a biblical scene should evoke.

I'll argue that the magi who appear in Matthew, just after Christmas, need to be a little funky in your film. Their hair, makeup, clothing, body art, jewelry, accents—all of it has to scream out, as the magi arrive in Jerusalem, "We're not from around here." And, yet, they seem to know exactly what they're doing there.

The word *magi* comes to us directly from the Greek word *magoi*, which can mean "magicians." They don't plan to saw anyone in half or produce rabbits from hats, however. "Sorcerers" might be more fitting. Or, more charitably, priests from a different religion. They're also astrologers, for they interpret the night sky. Scholars debate where in "the east" they reside; they could be from Arabia or perhaps they're Zoroastrian clerics from Persia (modern Iran). No one would mistake them for Jews, especially since they've been reading the stars. They could be living examples of the practices that Deuteronomy 18:9-14 explicitly forbids: augury and divination. But somehow their "foreign" wisdom leads them to discover what King Herod and the Jewish chief priests and scribes don't know: the king of the Jews has been born and deserves their adoration.

Nothing about Matthew's portrait of the magi criticizes them. Nothing treats them as dolts or sinners. In fact, their precious gifts recall scenes in Isaiah 60:1-6 and Psalm 72:10-11. At one level, then, they've been expected. As outsiders from another land, they also anticipate the commission Jesus gives his followers to go to "all nations" (28:19; recall chapter 4). Maybe most striking: they bravely choose sides when the story turns sinister.

In chapter 5 we explored Pilate's behavior at Jesus's sham trial. The beginning of Matthew's narrative, where the magi make their entrance, features a different despot. Herod the Great, a powerful local king who ruled on behalf of Rome, responds with fear when the magi tell him about the Messiah's birth. Immediately after the magi leave the story, after they courageously disobey Herod's command to reveal Jesus's location, Herod orders a murderous rampage to eliminate the infants and toddlers in Bethlehem and the surrounding region

(2:16). Something about the arrival of God's kingdom makes rulers, those who benefit the most from the status quo, quick to protect what's theirs. Christmas, in Matthew's view, begins to stir hopes of a political reckoning, or maybe an upheaval. Admittedly, they don't play Christmas carols about revolution during December in the mall. Matthew hums to a different playlist.

The magi grasp something of what Herod nervously perceives, that this young king's birth will eventually upend the world. That's because God protects them through a dream. Through the magi's story, we remember that Christmas heralds a new world order coming, accomplished by God.

The magi's appearance also declares that truth can come from unexpected sources. To return to my fantasies about being a filmmaker, I don't want the magi to prompt giggles. I won't depict them as foreigners in ways that traffic in racist themes or xenophobia. I want their stark "otherness," as measured by the dominant culture's point of view, to make a statement: no one person, tradition, or group gets to claim a monopoly on the truth. The magi, consulting their own sources of wisdom and following their own practices, manage to get very close to Jesus. All it takes is a quick consultation of Scripture (v. 6, referring to Micah 5:1, 3, and 2 Samuel 5:2) to aim them toward the right house. Don't presume to limit where or how God can be glimpsed.

In our current context, a perceived decline in the vitality of Christian congregations leads some people to grow increasingly self-protective or to imagine themselves as though they must compete aggressively for a viable share in a religious "marketplace" (which is a terrible term to describe what we're talking about). The insight, humility, generosity, and courage of the magi can encourage us to listen carefully to our neighbors, to learn from their traditions, and to discover how they perceive both the valuable parts and the shortcomings of our religion.

The church was never meant to exist as a bastion to protect doctrinal purity. We shouldn't treat the church as a community charged to preserve and police a narrow understanding of what it means to belong. Yes, theology matters. At the same time, Jesus has so little to say in Matthew about exactly what he wants people to believe. We might learn a thing or two from so-called outsiders. They might help us stay focused on the mercy and welcome that reside at the heart of Jesus's ministry.

Matthew 13:24-30, 36-43

(Weeds Interspersed among Wheat)

It's ironic. Matthew brims with promised judgment, yet it warns us of the dangers of rushing to judgment ourselves. Our priority should remain, instead, to nourish faith and empower people who are vulnerable.

I want to talk about films one more time. The *Blade Runner* movies revolve around a predicament that shows up in numerous works of science fiction: what would we do if dangerous androids or artificially created human beings dwelled among us? In the *Blade Runner* universe, engineered "replicants" infiltrate population centers. They look identical to real human beings, although their hidden strength and psychology make them a threat to society at large. They therefore need to be hunted, identified, and destroyed (or "retired" in the films' lingo). The imposters' presence gives voice to a kind of primal human fear. What if we can't trust the people around us? What happens to civilization if neighbors who seem to be just like us turn out to be dangerous?

Matthew, as we've discussed, has a habit of passing along stories about God sorting things into two groups. That's probably because the Gospel first influenced communities that were buzzing with distrust. They weren't concerned with replicants, of course, but with people they feared could prove disruptive to their own ability to live faithfully. Possibly some of Matthew's first readers were tempted to get the sorting started themselves, taking the responsibility into their own hands. Apparently, they suspected that even more folks would let them down. Better to identify them before the damage is done, the reasoning goes. You can easily imagine how those distrustful reflexes arise from fear, anger, oppression, or unhealed wounds from previous disagreements.

We've discussed Matthew's interest in depicting Jesus and his ministry as a promise about a coming reckoning, in which the truth will be told. We've explored the way this Gospel imagines judgment and punishment. We've delved into parables about dividing sheep and goats (25:31-46, recall chapter 1) and dividing the things found in the sea (13:47-50, recall chapter 2). Now here's one about separating out weeds that look like and grow alongside wheat.

Jesus takes extra time to interpret this parable, which is unusual. His interpretation treats the parable as an allegory about the need to wait for him ("the Son of Man") to take care of the sorting when "the end of the age" finally arrives. Almost all of Matthew 13 makes up one of Jesus's five long speeches in Matthew. We were in the midst of this speech previously when we explored the parable of the dragnet in chapter 2.

Jesus describes the field as a microcosm of an epic struggle between him and "the evil one," meaning the devil. The devil bears responsibility for a fiendish plan to sow counterfeits among the authentic, grain-bearing plants.

Faith can be a fragile thing, whether it's "little faith" or maturing faith.

The owner of the field shows great wisdom, however, in commanding that both wheat and weeds be allowed to grow together. Anyone who zealously tears out the weeds will uproot the wheat.

Faith can be a fragile thing, whether it's "little faith" or maturing faith. The need to give faith an environment to survive and grow outweighs other concerns, at least in this parable's logic.

The time will come to destroy the useless weeds, but that task belongs to the reapers, whom Jesus likens to angels specially sent to do God's bidding. Everyone else should proceed carefully. That doesn't mean a lack of concern about wickedness nor a refusal to hold people accountable for their actions. It means that judgment, whatever it will look like, is God's responsibility.

Once again, we encounter disturbing images, including a "furnace of fire" and "weeping and gnashing of teeth." Yet we should be careful not to assume hastily that we know exactly whom or what Jesus has in mind. You might secretly wish he's referring to the couple who occasionally sit in the pew in front of you—you know, the ones who scroll through their phones during the sermon and never put anything in the offering plate. At this point in our study of Matthew, however, it should be clear that we mustn't conclude that God's judgment is about getting rid of the people who annoy us or who don't measure up to our standards of "proper" behavior. The parable describes a cosmic struggle, not the petty offenses we hold on to.

Look again at what goes into the furnace: "all causes of sin and all evildoers." A more literal translation is "all the stumbling blocks and the ones who perform lawlessness" (v. 41, author's translation). Jesus uses similar "stumbling block" vocabulary in 18:6-7 when he warns about whatever causes other people, especially unwitting people, to fall into sin or struggle. Interpreting the parable, Jesus singles out the powers that *cause* sin—things like greed, fear, and hatred. He means the things that lead people into waywardness—like lies and contempt. He means the pressures that turn a person's life from a promising journey into a desperate slog for survival—like racist policies, family dysfunctions, addiction, and cycles of poverty. We could make a long list.

The parable and Jesus's interpretation assume a universe in which human beings and the choices we make aren't the only powers in play. He's concerned about spiritual harm, social forces, hopelessness, noxious politics, debilitating grief, and cruelty. He promises to do away with them. Then they'll no longer hurt people. The parable promises a time when our existence will be made safe, allowing everyone to bear fruit.

What I appreciate about this parable is the initial impulse on the farm: let's rid the field of the weeds. The desire to leap into action speaks to my own frustrated inclination to discredit other people who bear the name *Christian*. If I could get rid of everyone I thought was counterproductive, I'd be busy. If I could run the church all by myself—or with a few handpicked friends—and if I could hold power over what my fellow Christians read, believe, do in their spare time, turn to for news, and watch on television, I think I could make the kingdom of God a lot more visible in the world. But, of course, the parable leads me to realize all the collateral damage I'd do in the process, uprooting plants that need careful tending, like I was a reckless gardener going berserk with a rototiller. Talk about a stumbling block!

In other words, I think this parable expresses concern about believers who think it's their responsibility to devise litmus tests to determine exactly who belongs. Or who deserves to be here. Or who sullies Jesus's reputation. Jesus doesn't imply that the church shouldn't speak out against evil, broken values, violence, unjust policies, and moral apathy. Especially in our modern times, congregations can be strong engines for advocacy and reform. What Jesus aims to steer us away from, however, is doing advocacy and reform in ways that sacrifice our paramount calling to be a community of people who act mercifully. When the church loses its way and refuses to leave promised judgment in God's hands, our capacity for compassion becomes the first casualty.

Congregations and individual Christians benefit when they look at the church's own history of impatience and divisiveness. Something made the earliest readers of this Gospel antsy, frustrated, and eager to see their rivals get what someone thought should be coming to them.

I don't know exactly what the "something" was, but their fixation on it probably didn't help anyone contribute to a more Christlike community. Tending the ground in which we and our spiritual siblings grow should be the primary concern. Various plants, some with less vitality than others, need that space if they're going to have a chance to flower.

Matthew 13:31-32
(From Mustard Seed to Tree)

The kingdom of heaven resembles a quirky tree sprouting up where it will. Maybe we'll find one growing already in places we haven't thought to look.

Many people know this parable. It's about a very tiny seed that nevertheless turns into something comparatively huge. The imagery illustrates the kingdom of heaven as something that originally germinates in relative obscurity, borne along by each of Jesus's sermons and healing, until one day it reaches maturity as a very distinctive tree.

There's more to the story. Jesus appears to have failed his Botany 101 class. Mustard seeds may be very small, but smaller seeds exist on earth. We needn't hold this against Jesus, since he didn't travel the globe studying plants. He still makes his point. Nevertheless, his comments about a mustard seed becoming a tree might have elicited some snickers from the assembled crowd for a different reason. Mustard seeds in Galilee grow into thick shrubs, but no one would consider them trees.

Forms of this parable appear also in Mark 4:30-32 and Luke 13:18-19. Matthew's version, however, ratchets up the satire, for it has Jesus calling the mature plant both "the greatest of shrubs" and "a tree." It's certainly not the latter. We should wonder why Jesus doesn't compare the Kingdom to something grand, like a cedar tree, especially since his brief parable recalls a passage from Ezekiel 17:22-24, which describes a lofty cedar that provides a home for birds. Cedars from Lebanon appear occasionally in the Old Testament as symbols of stability and fascination. But Jesus, with tongue in cheek, imagines the Kingdom as something more homely: "the greatest of shrubs." In fact, the Greek word translated "shrubs" more commonly means simply "vegetables." Never let anyone convince you that humor is beneath Jesus's dignity. He knows the power of understatement, both for getting a laugh and for making his case.

Leave it to kings to construct impressive buildings from precious cedars (1 Kings 5:6). Jesus and his band of misfits from the undesirable side of town boast of their movement as a compact shrub. If you want to see the kingdom of heaven in all its glory, don't look for symbols of wealth and status. It's never the shiny new thing or the trendy invention. It's the place where life flourishes, growing thickly and reproducing quickly, as mustard plants do. People sometimes compare wild mustard to a weed, because it easily spreads, grows dense, and crowds out other vegetation, but mustard also has medicinal qualities. It might not be a cash crop, but that doesn't mean it lacks value. It promotes health.

Plus, the birds like it. The mature plant Jesus describes doesn't exist just for show. Inside its branches it creates a habitat, providing shelter for birds and their young. Every chirp from a hatchling associates the Kingdom with peace, relief, and delight. Creatures that find themselves vulnerable in the open thrive safely within its reach.

If the Kingdom resembles a mustard plant, that means it will grow wherever it can sink a tiny root into the ground. It won't stay put where the landscapers want it to stay. It will mess with our expectations and sometimes embarrass us a little. "Why, yes, that is a mustard plant growing in my yard. I know azaleas are prettier and better for property values, but that thing just won't go away. Anyway, it keeps attracting birds that sing like they're really glad to live there."

This playful if not flippant parable asks us to focus on what's important about the Kingdom: it makes room for life to prosper. If we extend this parable's imagery, maybe we shouldn't talk about the church as a community as much as an ecosystem, a place where all work together to ensure one another's well-being. Calling the church a family in our era is problematic, I think, because it promises a depth of relationship and mutual care that few congregations can provide. Not everyone wants another imperfect family, to be honest. Nor are churches businesses that think in terms of products, outcomes, and returns on investments. Mercy and refuge refuse to be measured easily.

People and leaders of numerous congregations yearn to "be relevant," hoping that the world will take notice of their programs and their message. For some groups in the church, their desire for relevance disguises their thirst for power and prominence. It's tempting, especially in our combustible culture, for churches to seek their survival or their ability to shape public opinion by force instead of through love and reconciliation. Power-hungry ambitions seek out cedar trees to build their majesty. An ecosystem church that truly includes everyone, so that everyone really belongs, will be content with the ragtag identity of a mustard shrub.

Matthew 27:25

(The Stain of Bloodguilt)

Reading Matthew should make us unable to forget that Christians need to remain committed to repairing damages that Christian theology—and we Christians ourselves—have caused to others. Distinctive aspects of this Gospel and recent surges in antisemitic incidents compel the church to remain attentive to our Jewish neighbors.

I've noted already how Matthew bears evidence of tensions and resentments that were simmering when this Gospel was composed. Not long after that time, "church" and "synagogue" understood themselves as separate and essentially mutually exclusive communities. Once the Christian movement became almost entirely a Gentile movement, many church leaders were quick to blame Jews for a host of matters, accusing them of rejecting God's blessings and being uniquely responsible for Jesus's death. Literally for centuries upon centuries, widely influential Christian theologians deployed anti-Jewish vitriol in their teachings. Hateful accusations and caricatures infected art, ritual, law, and popular attitudes. You can draw a line connecting the kind of critical language we find in Matthew, as well as in other New Testament writings, all the way to the antisemitism of our time.

I'm not suggesting that the author of Matthew would be pleased with the ways Christians have treated Jews and Judaism with contempt. I simply don't know what the author would think. Pondering the degree to which this Gospel itself is anti-Jewish is a separate question. My emphasis here is a more immediately alarming truth: Christians have been guilty of mining Matthew for material to fuel their anti-Jewish opinions and behaviors. When we take, for example, Jesus's complaints about religious hypocrisy as an authoritative word on Jewish beliefs and practices as a whole, we're guilty of misappropriating and sharpening the teachings that Matthew reports (recall the discussion of 23:1-36, in chapter 5).

Christians have been guilty of mining Matthew for material to fuel their anti-Jewish opinions and behaviors.

When we examined how Matthew depicts Pilate (also in chapter 5), I noted that the crowd of assembled Jews in Jerusalem, having been influenced by their authorities (27:20), declare to Pilate, "His [Jesus's] blood be on us and on our children!" (27:25). Their words end the trial, for Pilate sends Jesus to his execution in the following verse. (Pilate alone had the jurisdiction to order Jesus's crucifixion.) What does the crowd mean by saying this, and what makes the crowd's shout a significant part of Matthew, which is the only Gospel that includes the line?

Most likely Matthew depicts the crowd as unintentionally offering a harrowing prophecy of the suffering that Jews in Jerusalem and the wider region would experience forty years later, when a revolt against the Romans culminated in the razing of the Jerusalem Temple in 70 CE. By including the crowd's statement, Matthew makes a subtle attempt to tell readers that rejecting Jesus would come with consequences. There's a disturbing theological insinuation at the heart of the matter, which is that the Jewish victims of the later war somehow got what they deserved, thanks to the actions of a handful of their ancestors. I personally find that kind of theology, one that blames victims, abhorrent and misguided. Does Matthew really mean it that way? We can't be sure, but I find this the most likely explanation of what's happening as Matthew narrates the trial. I can't defend that theological point of view and I don't accept it. I don't say that because I think I'm especially enlightened, but instead because other parts of the Bible lead me to understand that God doesn't operate that way. It would take a separate book to explain why.

The controversy surrounding this verse about Jesus's "blood" gets worse, I'm afraid. For most of Christian history, there have been teachers and preachers who interpreted the crowd's shout as a "blood curse" that covers all Jews. The idea goes that Matthew understands the crowd to be accepting the guilt for Jesus's death and also extending it to their children, meaning all Jews in all times and places. As a result, some Christians have called Jews "Christ-killers" who are always the enemy of faith, because their hands are forever stained with the Messiah's blood.

If there's a stain surrounding this verse, it's on the church's hands. The history that encompasses this verse doesn't wash away. The crowd's cry, heard today in our current context, should call to mind the violence that always springs from anti-Judaism and its more modern manifestation, antisemitism. Hostility toward Judaism, Christianity's spiritual sibling, remains the church's original sin.

I'm not suggesting we cut this verse out of the Bible. That wouldn't solve anything, and then we'd be tempted never to put down our scissors. Rather, I urge us to consider this verse as a summons to remember the ways that theology can be weaponized against people—not just Jews alone. When I read the verse it prompts me to read Matthew as if I'm observing a family argument from the late first century. It's hardly a superficial argument, but one about very important matters. Old arguments, whether left alone or restoked over generations, usually require interventions. We all bear responsibility to help the church repair damage that has been done and work toward a reconciled future.

Once, during a discussion about similar biblical passages, a friend of mine who is a rabbi commented that all religions have committed mistakes—sometimes deep ethical offenses—that they need to acknowledge and repair. He also counseled that it's impossible to erase those errors. Repudiating something or disavowing an idea doesn't make it go away, he insisted. He's right. We compound our trespasses when we think, "Well, we denounced *that*, so now let's move on and pretend it didn't happen." Don't ignore it. Unsavory parts of our shared history and memory continue to call out to us, like Abel's blood crying to God from the ground in Genesis 4:10. Those voices from the past ask us to remember. When we do so, and when we work toward repairs, we're less likely to make the same mistake again. It's a tangible sign of progress toward reconciliation.

Many aspects of Matthew can inspire the church to be more merciful. May the enduring stain that intensifies and tarnishes this verse be one of them.

Reflections

Even with all of Matthew's complexity and intensity, I think in the end it expresses a relatively straightforward message to people who want to follow Jesus and participate in the blessings he brings: Matthew begs us to avoid distractions. The life of faith entails staying fixed on Jesus and participating in his life-giving ministry. That's the story.

Don't forget, I said "straightforward," not "easy." Faith has a way of being complicated. We find ourselves in crowded soil, eager to avoid having our roots undermined by the afflictions, trials, disappointments, and unfairness that can materialize without warning. To take Matthew seriously involves recognizing our dependence on Jesus and his compassion, our need for one another, and our imperative not to make the life of faith more weighty and exhausting for anyone else.

Matthew's message about avoiding distractions strikes me as straightforward because it recognizes that distractions threaten faith— both mine and others'. When we're preoccupied with threats it becomes impossible for wonder and joy to bloom. Insisting on being right and claiming the authority to judge others make it impossible to show compassion. Rooting out villains opens the door to violence that cannot be undone. All of it gets in the way of the blessings Jesus promises in the first words of his first sermon.

What about the intensity residing between the lines in Matthew? It inscribes into our Scriptures long-standing memories about ancient yet persistent divisions. When people fight over theology, influence, leadership, and power, they usually forget how to act mercifully. They usually neglect the people most in need of mercy. Division brings distraction. Distraction results in damage. Matthew brings a deep urgency to the topic. This Gospel doesn't want anyone to miss out on the opportunity to benefit from Jesus's blessings and to play a part in seeing them spread far and wide. That's the straightforward part.

Jesus asks us to lay power and dominion aside and instead imitate his relentless gentleness and loving-kindness.

The distractions that Jesus warns about may still cause damage. Some of us grow too convinced that we're right and that good ideas can't come from outside our traditions, systems, doctrines, or prejudices. Some of us are quick to anoint ourselves as the ones qualified to do the truth-telling that only God can do. Some of us can't get over a fascination with strength and a willingness to use our power to steamroll others. Our disappointments lead us to blame our neighbors and slander their reputations. These various distractions bear one thing in common, in that they all imagine the church to be an instrument of God's power and dominion on earth. To the contrary, Jesus asks us to lay power and dominion aside and instead imitate his relentless gentleness and loving-kindness. Like I said, it's straightforward but hardly easy.

Afterword

Joining Jesus in the Uproar

Jesus talks a lot in Matthew, which is why our exploration has focused more on what he teaches than on what he does in this Gospel. If you prefer encountering Jesus in a setting where he says little and cultivates greater mystery, you'll love the Gospel of Mark. Every Gospel has its own story to tell. Every Gospel wants to shape its audience's impressions.

In speaking so frequently in Matthew, Jesus raises many hopes with the promises he makes. He announces the dawning of new realities. He pledges to lift up those who have been pushed down. He extols the transformative power of forgiveness. He also gets our attention with his spoken criticisms and warnings. Matthew presents him as someone with a lot to announce, a teacher worth your time.

Effective teaching, however, relies on more than long speeches, pointed warnings, and clever parables. You'll never lecture people into joining Jesus's movement. If we want to be transformed by the blessings he promises, we need to do more than read or listen carefully and take careful notes. He invites us to take steps, too.

Matthew 14:28-32

(Walk on the Water)

Matthew, Mark, and John all tell about a time when Jesus's followers spot him walking across the sea while they struggle to get their boat safely to shore during a windstorm. The sight of him striding along the water terrifies them, and understandably so. Finally, out of the dim light he identifies himself and tells them not to fear.

Only Matthew extends the story with a description of Peter joining Jesus on the water. Matthew doesn't reveal what motivates Peter to say, "Lord, if it is you, command me to come to you on the water" (v. 28). Does Peter still think he's seeing a ghost? Is he showing off and somehow trying to distinguish himself from his peers in the boat? Does his request signal a lack of trust and a desire to make demands of Jesus? Maybe the excitement and relief overwhelm him. I'd be discombobulated myself.

Jesus doesn't criticize Peter's request, so I think we shouldn't either. Peter says what he says in good faith. At some basic level, Peter knows there's security with Jesus, so he'd rather be *with* Jesus than in the rickety, waterlogged boat. Jesus seems fine with it. Instead of launching a mini-sermon about the importance of trusting from a distance, Jesus simply welcomes Peter: "Come," he says. Experience.

And there goes Peter, stepping onto the choppy waves, across the sea and all the unruly peril it represents in the Bible's perspective (for example, Psalm 104:5-9). A glorious experience starts to take shape with each step, until a sharp gust seizes Peter's attention and the fear comes back. Fear weighs down everything. Peter starts sinking. Jesus grabs him before the waves swallow him and returns him to the boat.

Jesus gently—and maybe joyfully—chides Peter for his "little faith." Peter's not quite there yet. Even with all his brashness, he's still on a journey. Faith is fragile. We can relate.

I appreciate that Peter's expression of little faith—which, remember, is really an expression of "little trust"—possesses enough strength to make him desire to step onto a tumultuous sea to meet Jesus, who's already out there. The trust that Peter expresses in this moment exceeds his confidence that he's really talking to Jesus and not a ghost. His trust exceeds his assurance that Jesus will keep him safe. Peter's trust dares to assert that new things are indeed possible with Jesus. Peter trusts that Jesus's power outweighs the chaos. He trusts that "what's possible" isn't what he once thought. Eventually he and Jesus's other followers will find that God's power in Jesus proves itself stronger than death itself.

If you ever get to travel to the Sea of Galilee, be sure to visit the Ginosar kibbutz and see the ancient boat that archaeologists pulled out of the mud in 1986 when the water level was particularly low. It doesn't look as seaworthy as I'd prefer. The design and technology appear no match for a serious storm. I understand the disciples' predicament, if that's the kind of vessel they have. Jesus doesn't show up on the water with a sturdier boat for them to ride. He shows up with the power to withstand the disorder. He's willing to be in the throes of threat and uncertainty. He doesn't permanently settle the sea. More storms will come. He'll be there again.

Jesus says, "Do not be afraid" in 14:27. That's like saying, "Stop worrying" or, "Cheer up." Easier said than done. Those words usually have little effect on their own, but being in the presence of the one who speaks them might change things. In other words, we'll need more than inspiring (or threatening) words to build the kind of trust that Jesus urges his people to have. We'll need some hands-on experience out there in the waves, joining Jesus himself in the thick of it all.

Jesus's Promised Blessings

The portrait Matthew draws of Jesus tells us where to find him. He promises to be present among those who experience spiritual poverty, those who mourn, those who are meek, and so on. He promises to be found when anyone extends mercy to a person who suffers and has been pulverized by their circumstances. He promises to show up in a community committed to reconciliation. He promises to accompany people when they go out to continue spreading his mercy and acceptance.

Peter's adventure on the Sea of Galilee indicates he *really* wants to know and *really* wants to experience the blessings Jesus provides. *Promised* blessings mean only so much. At the end of the day, we need actualized blessings to satisfy the world's hunger.

Matthew reassures its readers that we can rely on this promise-making Jesus.

Matthew reassures its readers that we can rely on this promise-making Jesus. But the Gospel's purpose goes beyond providing written assurances. It exhorts us to experience him for ourselves. Our exploration of Matthew can encourage us to put ourselves among the places and people where Jesus's mercy makes a difference. It also admonishes us to give up the disputes, fears, pettiness, and hypocrisy that get in the way of Jesus's work—the things that create stumbling blocks for others. The howling wind and the threatening waves make a lot of noise. We even stir up some of the storms ourselves. But they won't drive Jesus away.

May we read Matthew in ways that honor its determination to keep us focused on what matters most and to keep us situated with Jesus and the blessings he brings with him.

For Further Reading

We've only skimmed the surface together. If you want to dive deeper into Matthew, here are a few books I think you'll find useful. I've organized the list from most accessible to more technical. If you're new to exploring the Bible on your own and want a resource that's readable, start with a book near the top of the list. If you're more comfortable with books written by biblical scholars that answer the kinds of questions that delight biblical scholars (I admit, we can be a strange bunch), especially questions about ancient history, society, language, and culture, try a book nearer the bottom of the list. Nothing I'm recommending here is extraordinarily dense or lost in the clouds. Each book that is marked with an asterisk (*) is considered a "commentary" on Matthew, meaning that those books walk through Matthew in sequence, from chapter 1 through chapter 28. That makes them useful to consult if you're working your way through Matthew from start to finish. Their comments will illuminate Matthew's details as you go.

* **Reid, Barbara E., O.P. *The Gospel according to Matthew*. New Collegeville Bible Commentary. Liturgical Press, 2005.**

This book is part of a series of biblical commentaries produced by Roman Catholic scholars. The author, who is a Dominican sister and a world-renowned New Testament scholar, offers basic and brief commentary on the story Matthew tells.

Taylor, Barbara Brown. *The Seeds of Heaven: Sermons on the Gospel of Matthew.* **Revised Edition. Westminster John Knox Press, 2004.**

Written by one of the most celebrated white American Protestant preachers of her generation, this book collects fifteen compelling sermons based on fifteen different passages from Matthew.

⋆ **Long, Thomas G.** *Matthew.* **Westminster Bible Companion. Westminster John Knox Press, 1997.**

I recommend this book highly because it communicates so much information in such a clear voice without technical language. The author, who is a minister in the Presbyterian Church (USA) and a retired professor of preaching, guides readers into Matthew's nuances and their relevance for reading this Gospel as good news.

⋆ **Uytanlet, Samson L. with Kiem-Kiok Kwa.** *Matthew: A Pastoral and Contextual Commentary.* **Asia Bible Commentary. Langham Global Library, 2017.**

The primary author is a professor at an evangelical biblical seminary in the Philippines and a pastor of an evangelical Filipino-Chinese church in Manila. His explanation of Matthew occurs in conversation with modern Asian cultural realities. That approach illuminates the fact that all of us find various points of connection and disconnection with the culture Jesus inhabited, depending on our own identities, values, and backgrounds.

⋆ **Case-Winters, Anna.** *Matthew.* **Belief: A Theological Commentary on the Bible. Westminster John Knox Press, 2015.**

In an inviting style, this book—written by a theology professor and minister in the Presbyterian Church (USA)—pauses its comments on the narrative occasionally to discuss how Matthew has informed and continues to inform various Christian beliefs and practices.

★ **Senior, Donald.** *Matthew.* **Abingdon New Testament Commentary. Abingdon Press, 1998.**

This perceptive commentary, written by an ecumenically minded Roman Catholic priest and New Testament scholar, offers useful insights on the historical context of the world Matthew describes, the literature that influenced the points of view we find in Matthew, and the theological claims of the Gospel.

In addition, I highly recommend a number of accessible and smart books written by Amy-Jill Levine, a New Testament scholar with a special gift for making complicated topics easy to understand. She's especially skilled at helping readers discover how Jesus's first-century Jewish contemporaries would have viewed him in light of their shared cultural and religious commitments. Several books in her Beginner's Guide series will take you further into Matthew, even if you don't consider yourself a "beginner." Of the five titles listed here, only the book on Jesus's Sermon on the Mount deals exclusively with Matthew. The other four will help you reflect on the kinds of material that all the Gospels, including Matthew, preserve about Jesus and the difference he makes for the world.

> *The Difficult Words of Jesus: A Beginner's Guide to His Most Perplexing Teachings.* Abingdon Press, 2021.
>
> *Entering the Passion of Jesus: A Beginner's Guide to Holy Week.* Abingdon Press, 2018.
>
> *Light of the World: A Beginner's Guide to Advent.* Abingdon Press, 2019.
>
> *Sermon on the Mount: A Beginner's Guide to the Kingdom of Heaven.* Abingdon Press, 2020.
>
> *Signs and Wonders: A Beginner's Guide to the Miracles of Jesus.* Abingdon Press, 2022.

Watch videos based on *Matthew* with Matthew L. Skinner through Amplify Media.

Amplify Media is a multimedia platform that delivers high quality, searchable content with an emphasis on Wesleyan perspectives for churchwide, group, or individual use on any device at any time. In a world of sometimes overwhelming choices, Amplify gives church leaders and congregants media capabilities that are contemporary, relevant, effective and, most importantly, affordable and sustainable.

With *Amplify Media* church leaders can:

- Provide a reliable source of Christian content through a Wesleyan lens for teaching, training, and inspiration in a customizable library
- Deliver their own preaching and worship content in a way the congregation knows and appreciates
- Build the church's capacity to innovate with engaging content and accessible technology
- Equip the congregation to better understand the Bible and its application
- Deepen discipleship beyond the church walls

Ask your group leader or pastor about Amplify Media and sign up today at www.AmplifyMedia.com.

Watch videos based on *Matthew* with Matthew L. Skinner through Amplify Media.

Amplify Media is a multimedia platform that delivers high quality, searchable content with an emphasis on Wesleyan perspectives for churchwide, group, or individual use on any device at any time. In a world of sometimes overwhelming choices, Amplify gives church leaders and congregants media capabilities that are contemporary, relevant, effective and, most importantly, affordable and sustainable.

With *Amplify Media* church leaders can:

- Provide a reliable source of Christian content through a Wesleyan lens for teaching, training, and inspiration in a customizable library
- Deliver their own preaching and worship content in a way the congregation knows and appreciates
- Build the church's capacity to innovate with engaging content and accessible technology
- Equip the congregation to better understand the Bible and its application
- Deepen discipleship beyond the church walls